Endorsements for Shape Your Soul

Finally! A book about an exercise I will love!! How often do you think about a spiritual workout? Did you know the Bible is full of encouragement to exercise our souls? In *Shape Your Soul*, Peggy Cunningham presents 31 cleverly-crafted devotionals presenting "soul exercises" for you to practice daily in the strength of The Great Physician. Each very biblically-sound devotional is well-seasoned with touching and sometimes astonishing personal accounts (many from her missionary-life in Bolivia), and chock full of suggestions for your spiritual growth and physical health. The challenging questions she asks will help you evaluate your own spiritual life. In addition to the spiritual workout, each devotional ends with a "Today's Exercise" in which she takes a spiritual exercise and suggest a correlating physical exercise.

~ **Shirley Crowder**
Christian Author & Speaker, and Biblical Counselor
Prayer Study Guide –A Companion to *Prayer: It's Not About You.* Pix-N-Pens Publishing, 2017.
www.sjcrowder@throughthelensofscripture.com

Shape Your Soul is a combination of exciting adventure story-telling, devotional reading, biblical instruction and overall inspiration to draw our hearts closer to God in trust and love. I love Peggy Cunningham's ability to draw us into her missionary life in a way we see the spiritual adventures God is using to strengthen our faith no matter where we live or how God has called us. I was inspired, strengthened and mesmerized. You will be also.

~ **Kathy Collard Miller**
author of over 50 books including
No More Anger: Hope for an Out-of-Control Mom
www.KathyCollardMiller.com

In her devotional *Shape Your Soul*, Peggy Cunningham takes us to Bolivia, where she and her husband serve as missionaries to the Quechua people. Her captivating stories show how God uses challenging events to stretch and shape us and build a faith that moves mountains. She writes, "We all desire to live purposeful, powerful, and productive lives to glorify God." In each chapter she presents a verse to ponder and a question for personal reflection, along with a suggested soul exercise and stretch to strengthen and equip Christ-followers to face fears and threats with confidence in God's miraculous protection and guidance. The author's sweet spirit overflows the pages of *Shape Your Soul*, reminding us God is always faithful.

~ **Dianne Barker**
Author, speaker, and radio host
www.diannebarker.com

Through stories of her adventures as a missionary in Bolivia, Peggy Cunningham gives us a condor-eye's view of God's miraculous provision. Every account encourages us to stretch and grow our faith muscles until we learn to expect the supernatural. "We weren't made to fit in; we were made to stand out," she says. If you're tired of the flabby spiritual life that doubt and fear have created, get ready to discover the secrets that will shape your soul into a mean machine for God's glory.

~ **Jeanette Levellie**
author of bestselling devotional
Two Scoops of Grace with Chuckles on Top
humor/inspirational speaker, and slave of four cats.

Peggy Cunningham has led an interesting life – and uses the compelling tales of her missionary experiences to build her readers' faith. I found myself riveted as I imagined traveling with her over dangerous mountain roads or holding my breath as soldiers with machine guns boarded our bus. This is one devotional book that you will have trouble putting down after completing your reading for that day. I know I did!

~ Julie Zine Coleman
author of
Unexpected Love: The Heart of God Revealed through Jesus' Conversations with Women (Thomas Nelson, 2013)

If you are a person, like me, who does not like to exercise and challenged to find time for daily spiritual workouts then *Shape Your Soul: 31 Exercises of Faith that Move Mountains* will motivate you to start getting in shape immediately. These short shots of adrenaline boosters to strength your physical and spiritual heart are addicting! Caution: You won't be able to put Peggy's Cunningham's book down. God's faith training program is "soul" easy and encouraging.

Annetta Dellinger
JOYologist
Author of 20 plus books
including *JOY-spirations for Caregivers*
www.annettadellinger.com

© 2020, 2019, 2018 Peggy Cunningham

ISBN-13 Paperback: 978-1-950318-14-8
ISBN-13 Hardcover: 978-1-950318-35-3
ISBN-13 Digital: 978-1-950318-15-5

All rights reserved. No part of this publication may be reproduced or transmitted in any form or by any means without written permission from the publisher.

All Scripture quotations, unless otherwise indicated, are taken from *The Holy Bible, English Standard Version.* Copyright © 2000, 2001 by Crossway Bibles, a division of Good News Publishers. Used by permission. All rights reserved.

Scripture quotations marked NLT are taken from the *Holy Bible, New Living Translation,* copyright © 1996, 2004. Used by permission of Tyndale House Publishers, Inc., Wheaton Illinois 60189, U.S.A. All rights reserved.

Scripture quotations marked THE MESSAGE are from *The Message,* copyright © Eugene H. Peterson 1993, 1994, 1995. Used by permission of NavPress Publishing Group.

Scripture quotations marked HCSB are taken from the Holman Christian Standard Bible®, Copyright © 1999, 2000, 2002, 2003 by Holman Bible Publishers. Used by permission. Holman Christian Standard Bible®, Holman CSB®, and HCSB® are federally registered trademarks of Holman Bible Publishers.

Scripture quotations marked (NIV) are taken from the Holy Bible, New International Version®, NIV®. Copyright © 1973, 1978, 1984 by Biblica, Inc.™ Used by permission of Zondervan. All rights reserved worldwide.

Scripture quotations marked NRSV are from the New Revised Standard Version of the Bible, copyright 1989, by the Division of Christian Education of the National Council of the Churches of Christ in the U.S.A. Used by permission. All rights reserved.

Published by Worthy Words Press
www.WorthyWordsPress.com

Dedication

In memory of Lewis "Fuzzy" and Joanne Harrer, my hometown-street neighbors who shared Jesus with me, so I will someday live throughout eternity with them on heaven's HOMETOWN-GOLDEN streets.

Joanne loved McDonald's—because of her, so do I. After Joanne went to heaven, Chuck and I shared many breakfasts at McDonald's with Fuzzy during our furloughs. Now that they're together in heaven, I like to imagine that just maybe they're enjoying a hamburger under Heaven's golden arches.

We miss them down here. But, because they shared Jesus with their neighbors, Chuck and I will one day be there with them for all eternity. Since they were Jesus' messengers to us, we can be His messengers in Bolivia, where our neighbors of a different color, language and culture hear the Good News.

In a real way, Fuzzy and Joanne were missionaries to Bolivia without applying for a passport or boarding a plane. Today, I follow their example of being a neighbor with a passion for souls and a desire to share Christ with those who don't know Him yet. They continue to inspire many—including me—to serve God with all our hearts.

Acknowledgements

Thank you, Tracy Ruckman, for your passion for perfection and for working tirelessly to reach the goal of godly publications. You inspire me to write God's message and attain my dream of serving God as a writer. I'm grateful to you for your guidance and for publishing my books so God can use them for His purposes.

Thank you, Julie-Allyson Ieron, for your hard work and excellent editing. *Shape Your Soul* is a reality because of your teaching, mentoring, and friendship. Working with you is a joyful journey and always a learning experience. Because of your godly example as a writer, I am motivated to keep writing for God.

Thank you, Chuck, you truly have the gift of helps and never hesitate to use it to benefit others. Thank you for your help in my writing journey and my teaching ministry for children, teens, and women. You never cease to help me reach my dreams to accomplish God's purpose for my writing. Through the good and hard times, it's been an incredible journey serving God with you all these years.

Contents

Meet the Not-so-Much-in-Shape Author 3

God's Image 7

God's Call 15

God's Family 23

God's Spirit 31

God's Faithfulness 41

God's Teenagers 47

God's Protection 51

God's Romance 57

God's Grandparents 63

God's Grandmothers 73

God's Will 83

God's Plans 91

God's Direction 97

God's Presence 105

God's Healing 111

God's Friends 119

God's Relationships 125

God's Humor	131
God's Heart	137
God's Voice	143
God's Nature	149
God's Workers	155
God's Dogs	163
God's Bread	167
God's Hand	173
God's Senior Citizens	179
God's Food	187
God's Strawberries	195
God's Angels	199
God's Funny Bone	207
God's Messengers	217
References	227
About the Author	228
Other Books by the Author	229

PREFACE

Meet the Not-so-Much-in-Shape Author

"For truly, I say to you, if you have faith like a grain of mustard seed, you will say to this mountain, 'Move from here to there,' and it will move, and nothing will be impossible for you."
Matthew 17:20

I'm Peggy. And I'm your not-so-much-in-shape author.

Mostly, I'm inclined to refrain from the physical exercises I mention in the pages to come. But I do walk, sit up, and occasionally stretch. I once went to an exercise class, but by the time I drove to the class, put on my leotards, got out my mat, and greeted everyone in the room, I succumbed to exhaustion and left.

For me, the hardest exercise I mention in this book is sleep. Now, you may not think of sleep as an exercise, but you will be surprised to find it is. Maybe that tidbit will encourage you to continue reading—at least until you quench your curiosity about sleep.

Let me offer this caution. Before and after doing

the soul exercises that follow, talk to The Great Physician. And by all means, talk to your earthly physician before attempting any physical exercises. I assure you, doing the physical exercises is only encouraged, *not* required. However, when it comes to the spiritual exercises I'll describe for you, those I urge you to practice along with me. I am on this journey with you to exercise our souls daily. On those days when I skip my spiritual workout, my soul suffers for lack of discipline. Yours does, too. And, by the way, I know the dreaded mountain of exercising can be grueling, so I made a few chapters shorter to give you some cool down and pause time here and there—for those hectic days. Occasionally, pausing is good for the body and soul. It gives time to reflect and pray. I want us to be careful to remember though, never to push the pause button on God.

So, get your spiritual mat and begin these soul-shaping exercises with your not-so-athletic author, to work out your faith and move mountains. I hope these heart-warming and sometimes hair-raising stories will captivate your adventurism and spark your desire for a life of growing faith.

Are you ready to get your soul in shape? We can do this together!

God's Image

We Can Move Mountains

I awake every morning on a small ranch and slip out of my cowgirl boots each night in the Andes Mountains of Bolivia—spectacular, I know. I don't ride a horse, but I do spoil two ponies daily with hugs and carrots. I don't have cows either, but a herd of them moo just beyond my fence. The mountains around me reach 14,000 feet. I can almost see heaven from my upstairs windows.

Our physical lives may take place miles apart, but our spirits are near if we share faith in Jesus. As I look over my slice of the Andes, I realize that I've seen God move mountains. In fact, God moving mountains explains exactly why I (a girl whose hometown is nestled in the hillsides of Pennsylvania, U.S.A.) find myself here in this beautiful land.

Whether you're at sea level or soar high on a mountain top, you probably have seen mountains move, too. I hope that as you come along with me to

God's Gym and exercise your faith muscles in these pages, you'll soon notice movable mountains in your path. Your mountains may be different than mine, but still, we experience the same kinds of struggles as we climb the mountain of spiritual maturity.

Who Am I?

I should tell you at this point that I'm a missionary, which is why I'm in Bolivia, South America. But please don't stop reading yet. I promise, I don't sit on a pedestal, and if I did, I'd soon fall off. Also, since I am accident-prone, I would never climb up on that pedestal for any reason. Most missionaries I know readily acknowledge that we can't measure up to the myth that we somehow soar through life on a magical flying carpet high above everyone else.

Please erase your physical image of the missionary woman of centuries past. I don't wear my hair in a bun and I turned in my long skirt and tennis shoes long ago for jeans and Mary Jane shoes, occasional heels, and recently cowgirl boots (my favorites, by far). I know the missionary image (myth) is expected of me, yet I break the mold. I seek God's guidance—intent on manifesting God's image on the outside and on the inside.

Are you willing to exercise your soul and break the mold expected of you? Wouldn't you rather emulate the image of God than an image expected of you by the world? Wouldn't you rather be the *real* you? Yes, the person God is transforming into His image.

Read on and exercise your soul with me on this quest to flee the fear of having to fit in. After all, we weren't made to fit in; we were made to stand out—a shining light stands out in the darkness. Let's shine light into this dark world! We're all in the process of maturity in Christ. I hope you'll continue with me on this journey to drop our masks and let Jesus shine through.

It's a Daily Choice

My book is written from a woman's view of the mission field and the role of the church in her life. But it is also written to all women (men too) in God's family—all of us who seek to grow in faith and journey daily with Him on this path to heaven. Because, whether you minister in a foreign land or on the home front, I'm pretty sure we all desire to live purposeful, powerful, and productive lives that glorify God.

I want to challenge you to serve the Lord at your current earthly address in your current homeland and to spur you on until your journey ends at your heavenly address. We all can experience miracles, supernatural encounters, and everyday blessings of living for God. Let's exercise on, drop the masks and live in freedom—free to live according to God's Word. Let's allow God to stretch us and warm us up to a life of honesty and daily soul exercising!

Warmup with Stretching

Just like you, I'm seeking to exercise my soul and draw closer each day to the One who transforms me into His image—desiring to know Him better by flexing my faith muscles even if it's painful. Just like physical exercise, if we keep at it the rewards are great, the pain subsides, and our muscles become strong. By developing discipline with spiritual exercises, we become conformed to God's image day-by-day.

Occasionally, we may need to take off our heels and slip on our running shoes—or maybe even hiking boots depending on the uphill climb—but don't give up until you hear from your Father in heaven, "Well done." Only then can we slip into soft cloud-like slippers and rest our beautiful feet forever. Until then, let's keep exercising our souls to conform to His image.

First, we ought to warm up with a stretch; it'll be our first exercise of faith together. Here goes. We begin by claiming Jesus' promise from Matthew 17:20, "For truly, I say to you, if you have faith like a grain of mustard seed, you will say to this mountain, 'Move from here to there,' and it will move, and nothing will be impossible for you." Belief to this extreme is certainly a stretch for most of us. But it's absolutely worth the effort. Trust me for now; soon we'll discover the truth of this together.

Take Shape

- ❖ **Verse to Ponder**:

    "Your unfailing love, O LORD, is as vast as the heavens; your faithfulness reaches beyond the clouds" (Psalm 36:5, NLT).

- ❖ **Question:**

    What's your seemingly unmovable mountain today? As you look at that mountain, what do you pray God will do with it? How might He use it to help you stretch your faith daily, monthly, yearly?

- ❖ **Today's Exercise**:

    We know from research that stretching our bodies improves flexibility and blood flow to the muscles. Similarly, when circumstances stretch our faith muscles, we become more flexible to God's Will. In fact, we'll find He uses the stretch exercise to shape our souls.

    As He stretches you, He may place in your heart a mountainous dream—be it a disciplined prayer life, Bible study, or actual mountain climbing. Stretch toward that mountain and in the strength God gives, move it!

Stretch your faith muscles to move the mountain of unbelief.

God's Call
Prelude to Ministry

I've faced the shadow of death a few times on the mission field and even the possibility of my children's deaths. I've had a machine gun pointed at my head. My family and I suffered (and lived) through tropical diseases, political uprisings, and bombs going off in our immediate vicinity. In fact, we still face those fearful situations. Yet this is where I desire to be, on this mountain serving God from a mission base we call *Rumi Rancho*.

Unless you are a foreign missionary or live in a developing country, you probably haven't experienced the exact same daily struggles. Although, I'm guessing you've faced a few scary situations, health problems, or sick children. Our locations may be miles apart, but our Christian journey is more the same than different. We all share the same spiritual struggles, and we all go step-by-step as we walk with God, and we all carry Christ's gospel to the world.

(Isn't that what a missionary is?)

When construction began at our ministry base, contractors had to remove many rocks from the site—small ones, large ones, and a few gigantic boulders. *Rumi* (pronounced *roomy*) is the Quechua word for *rock*. It became obvious we were building on a rock mountain, and the name *Rumi Rancho* seemed appropriate. (Quechua is the language spoken in the area and Jesus is our Rock. It's His story we came to spread to the mountains and valleys nearby.)

I like to refer to it as our *holy* mountain because holy things happen here. Many meet their Savior on this ground where I live and work. They receive eternal life and a forever home in heaven. Underprivileged children learn practical skills they otherwise have no opportunity to learn. Even better, they learn about Jesus—many for the first time.

As for me, God has answered my prayers from His holy mountain in heaven and blessed my holy mountain on earth. Psalm 3:4 says, "He answers me from His holy mountain" (HCSB). He answered my husband's and my prayers and did miracles to bring us to this mountain we love. We still marvel at God's guidance, protection, provision, and His perfect plans. I hope as I tell you these real-life stories of how God has brought us to this place in time, He'll use them to stretch your faith so that He can and will move mountains for you.

God's Training Program

After I'd married my high school sweetheart, we moved thousands of miles from our small hometown in western Pennsylvania. It was the beginning of God's training for what He had planned for us in ministry. Even though I'd never been away from home before getting married, Chuck and I spent four years traveling with his military assignments until we returned to our place of birth after his tour of duty. He entered his father's business and climbed to the community's prestigious position of President of the Chamber of Commerce. Although he began to assume the role of business owner, God had a higher calling in mind. Our Heavenly Father wanted him in *His* business—winning souls around the world.

We were groomed for a life of success in the business while serving God in our church. We were the most unlikely missionaries. The thought of the Cunninghams leaving the comforts of home for the wilds of the mission field shocked many. Most who knew us believed it a passing whim. Even *we* questioned our qualifications. In our case, this Jim Elliott quote applied: "God doesn't call the qualified; He qualifies the called."

We've served in various capacities over our thirty-seven years in mission work. We've been dorm parents to high school girls at a mission school where my husband was also business manager. He has also served as director for two different missions. We hosted teams from the U.S.A. and managed a home for missionaries who did jungle surveys to locate unreached tribes. At times, my husband traveled to remote areas while I held down ministry in the city. I filled in as the librarian at two mission schools—one in the city and another in the lowlands of Bolivia. Yes, God does qualify the called and yes, missionaries wear many hats and need God's wisdom and enabling to fulfill His call.

Then as quickly as He'd called us, God changed our direction. It wasn't an easy transition, but He led us on the journey of our dreams—to work with the Quechua people. He led us to found Rumi Rancho Ministries. He nestled us in the Andes Mountains on a piece of stunning property, perched at 8,500 feet above sea level.

Prelude of Praise

This fast-forward summary of where we've been in these years of ministry is a prelude of the praises to God that we've sent up. *Praise* implies glory, honor, and worship; it leads us to exalt, reverence, magnify, give thanks to, and venerate our Lord. Actually, that definition summarizes the purposes I hope this book will accomplish in your life.

I'm not espousing the pros or cons of missionary work, nor is this a book to instruct those embarking on a missionary career. But rather, I write to extol the incredible and marvelous works of God—miracles, healings, and amazing answers to prayer—in my life and the lives of those around me. But if somewhere on these pages God calls you to serve Him in a faraway country, to support His work from the home front, or to follow His unique call on your life, I'd be humbled for my writing to be used of God in such a way.

I can tell you that the people who questioned our qualifications to be missionaries were right to do so. We weren't qualified (still aren't in our strength), but God allows us to do the impossible through Him. It is God who enables us, so He receives the glory. We depend on His promise in 1 Thessalonians 5:24 daily, "The one who calls you is faithful; he will surely do it."

So, let the stories that follow remind you that the God we serve is the God of all glory who miraculously invites us to have a relationship with Him. And He is the God of miracles who still answers prayers. Whether you're taking your first step with Him today, or you've been stepping with Him for years, just keep on stepping!

Take Shape

- ❖ **Verse to Ponder**:

    "Strength! Courage! Don't be timid; don't get discouraged. GOD, your God, is with you every step you take" (Joshua 1:9 MSG).

- ❖ **Question:**

    What steps are you taking today to grow a firm faith?

- ❖ **Today's Exercise:**

    Stepping improves balance and stability. A baby wobbles when he takes his first steps, but step-by-step with practice and help, he gains his balance and stands firm. Step-by-step our soul muscles stabilize and become firmly shaped. Step out! God will help you balance and keep you from falling! He is with you!

Stepping with God moves the mountain of instability.

God's Family
It's a Real Trip

Missionary children go along with their parents —like it or not—to the ends of the earth. When we announced to our families that God called us from our cozy life near relatives to the mission field far, far away, what do you think was the first response from their lips? You probably guessed it. "What about the children?" At the time, our daughter was two and our son nine. "You can't take our grandchildren to a dangerous country." In other words, it's okay for you to go but not them. How's that make you feel?

Our enthusiasm about becoming missionaries couldn't make room for all the concern. But now, having grandchildren of our own, I can relate. They live in California, and we consider *that* a faraway place with different customs.

After a two-year training course followed by a year of language school, we arrived on the field for the first time. Just about immediately, I realized the dangers that lurked about and my concern for my children increased. The words of the grandparents echoed in my ears—*What about the children?*

Culture Shock

Within a few months of our arrival, the four of us traveled to a remote area of Bolivia. It would be a time for us to experience the life and ministry of missionaries serving among the tribes. We hoped it would help us relate to missionary children at the school where we worked. My heart did flip-flops thinking of the dangers waiting.

As we boarded the filthy, outdated train to the regions beyond civilization, my daughter looked up into my eyes and asked, "Where are we going mommy?" The tight grip of her tiny hand caused me to wonder if she feared being lost among the crowd of Spanish-speaking passengers. I reassured her as our family boarded the train. "We're going to visit missionaries who live with an Indian tribe. We'll be there in a few hours." This seemed to satisfy her for the moment. I didn't mention the dangers we might encounter or the uncomfortable trip we were about to experience.

The whiff of live animals caught our nostrils as we searched for our assigned seats. We found them occupied by chickens and pigs. My husband shooed them to another part of the train car to find their owners, and we plopped into the hard seats. We noticed people on the top of the train catching a free ride. This wasn't like any commuter train we'd ridden in the States. With a jerk and roar of the engine, we left the city behind. It didn't take long for the rickety train to reach a speed that could have blown those poor souls right off the roof into the night air.

And so we rode, all night long. The children drifted off, but Chuck and I kept exchanging glances, wondering exactly what God was calling us to do.

In the early morning, the train stopped at our destination. Clutching our baggage, we leaped from the train just before it chugged off. We stood alone on hot, sandy ground. Towering cacti surrounded us for miles. They seemed to reach to the sky and bloomed with lacy white flowers. The wind whipped around our sweaty bodies as we gazed up and down the tracks hoping to see someone, anyone, who could get us to the mission.

It was a scene out of *Butch Cassidy and the Sundance Kid.* We were at the ends of the earth longing to see another human being searching for us. There we stood, four aliens nearly dropped out of the sky—stranded, with no one in sight to meet us.

My daughter's sweaty body inched close as we sat on a dusty rock. "Do you think the missionaries forgot us Mommy?"

"No sweetie, they'll be here soon." Inwardly I feared they *had* forgotten us; I hoped my voice didn't betray that fear. The music of birds tweeting and parrots chattering calmed my nerves, but the faint whistle of the train far down the track allowed no turning back.

Finally, after we'd waited a few hours in the scorching heat, the racket of a sputtering vehicle in the distance gave me hope that help was on the way. Finally, the missionary family arrived in a rusty truck that took us to their house, where we were met by scantily clad Indians. They welcomed us by caressing my daughter's blonde hair with calloused brown fingers and chatting in their native language.

Citizens of Heaven

Our month-long visit began with an introduction to the tribal village that became one of my most memorable moments. We groped through a jungle path in the moonlight to the Indian village to help deliver a baby. Haunting thoughts lurked in my mind. I wondered what shocking stories the trees around me would tell if they could talk.

When we entered the hut, the stench was overwhelming— there was garbage everywhere. In a dark corner, the mother-to-be lay on the mud floor. On these same grounds, decades before, five missionaries were killed. I knew some of the attackers were still living in the tribe. I had no reason for fear, though, because many had accepted the Lord as Savior and were new creations.

How would these Indians have heard the Good News if someone hadn't come to tell them (Romans

10:14)? They wouldn't have! They heard because of the ultimate sacrifice of five missionaries.

I transitioned from a missionary that night to a sister-in-Christ with a tribe of former assassins. I had arrived at the ends of the earth, and there I began to appreciate the universal family of God.

My daughter's fears vanished, as did mine. She joyfully played with the Indian children, rode their horses, and returned to civilization with boils on her behind from riding horses bareback. The marks and sores vanished, but the impression of that trip will last forever on her heart and mine. She made the transition, as we all did, from a child of civilization to a citizen of heaven, where all are the same in God's sight.

Have you made that transition? It's life changing!

God Equips

You don't have to cross an ocean to experience opposition or dangers to you and your family when you serve God. When God calls, don't hang up because of the circumstances around you. Don't run, just walk with Him. If He calls you to a job for Him, He will do it through you. God will empower you and strengthen your heart for the journey. He is your Transition Guide, and He will guide you step-by-step through life's changes and transitions.

Take Shape

- ❖ **Verse to Ponder:**
  "My health may fail, and my spirit may grow weak, but God remains the strength of my heart; he is mine forever" (Psalm 73:26 NLT).
- ❖ **Question:**
  What keeps you from walking in God's power today?
- ❖ **Today's Exercise:**
  Walking is recommended for many health issues including our heart muscles. In the same way, walking with God strengthens and shapes our spiritual hearts.

Walking with God moves the mountain of weakness.

God's Spirit
Machine Guns and Sleeping Ghosts

When I surrendered my life for service on a foreign field, I knew the possibilities of contracting tropical diseases, being bitten by venomous snakes, being subjected to prison or even dying. But actually living in a foreign country? That was the greater challenge.

The cultural adjustment intensified on the day armed soldiers surrounded my son and me, waving machines guns near our heads. Maybe I should back up and set the scene for you.

Typhoid Fears

Our son Chuck, then fifteen, contracted typhoid fever at the mission school where we worked. We were afraid he was going to die, since we had no way to get him to the city hospital, eight hours away. Torrential rains were falling all over Bolivia, making it impossible for the mission plane to reach the school. Since many roads and bridges had been washed away, we couldn't reach the city by land either.

A few days later the rains began to let up, but the mission radio couldn't make contact with mission headquarters in the city. Thankfully, we had a ham radio. Using it, we made contact, and a mission plane was sent to our aid.

After two weeks of treatment in a city hospital, he was released and we began our return to the school in a bus that looked a hundred years old. My son, sitting next to me, was still weak and looking frail after losing nearly thirty pounds.

I was concerned the trip would cause him to relapse. The conditions of the roads and the buses were deplorable. Often there were landslides and roadblocks and mechanical problems with the buses.

More Immediate Fears

On the small bus, people were carrying their chickens and pigs to sell in the market place, and the driver seemed to be in a race with other bus drivers to see who could go the fastest over dangerous roads. All of this was not exactly helpful for a teenaged passenger recovering from a life-threatening disease.

The bus chugged up to 14,000 feet on the dirt road. As it reached the pinnacle of the mountain, I marveled at God's creation. It was like being on top of the world.

But then the old bus began to pick up speed down the mountain. Glancing out the window, I was looking at the edge of the road with thousand-foot or more drop-offs, no guardrails, and a crazed driver at the wheel. It may have been called the Pan-American Highway, but it was more like a back road cut in the side of the mountain.

When we entered a mountain village, the bus stopped abruptly. I saw Quechua Indian ladies in their native dress selling fruit and bread. They were trying to get our attention by shouting out in Spanish the items they had for sale.

The mountain air was crisp—a welcome relief from the hot and humid climate in the lowlands, where we had been for two weeks—but the dust and thin air had me gasping for breath.

Then I was gasping for another reason: Suddenly, out of nowhere, uniformed military men with machine guns surrounded the bus. Now we were facing another problem: the military was detaining the bus to search for drugs and check our IDs.

It was our first year in Bolivia and everything was still new and strange to us. The trip was the first time I had traveled without the whole family by my side—my husband and daughter were waiting for us back at the mission school. My son was calm beside me, but he didn't realize we didn't have any form of identification with us. Our passports were in the capital city of La Paz to process our permanent visas, and we were left with nothing to identify us. Normally, people with no proof of permission to be in the country were arrested and taken to the nearest prison; this was especially true for foreigners.

Prison Conditions

Just a few weeks earlier, I had visited a prison in this underdeveloped country. I went with a group of missionary ladies to visit a young American lady who'd been arrested as she was leaving the country with cocaine in her possession.

The prison trip had been shocking. The smells were horrific and the living conditions appalling. Her cell had only a concrete floor, with no bathroom or bed, and she had nothing but the clothes on her back. Her only meals were what people from the outside brought to her.

The lady had no one to help her, so a ministry began as we took food, clothes, and God's Word to her each day, meeting her needs in every way we could. She came to know the Lord and began witnessing to the other prisoners, a ministry within a ministry. Eventually, she was extradited to the United States and left Bolivia a new creation in Christ.

That prison scene was on my mind. What would happen when the military men discovered we had no identification to show them? Would we be taken to a prison?

I told my son the problem we faced and we decided that the only thing we could do was pray. I said, "Put your head down, close your eyes and pretend you are sleeping. Don't open your eyes unless they insist. We are going to pray they don't see us."

My son looked at me as though I had lost my mind, but I assured him God would take care of us.

I glanced down the aisle once more and saw at least ten soldiers with machine guns. That didn't give me much peace. I prayed that God would put a hedge around us and that we would be overlooked. Even as I prayed, I knew I was asking the impossible. How could they miss two tall blondes with white skin in a bus filled with short people who had black hair and dark skin?

One by one people on the bus were checked—their luggage, their bodies, and their possessions. We could hear the baggage being taken out of the compartment underneath the bus. Every inch of the bus was searched.

We kept our heads down and our eyes shut.

We were in the middle of the bus and as they came down the aisle, I could hear their questions. They spoke with authority and sounded especially intimidating.

They came closer. The people sitting in front of us were asked to step into the aisle and were searched. The baggage over our heads was taken down, searched, and returned to the compartment.

My heart was racing. I couldn't tell if my son was breathing. He was absolutely silent.

I opened one eye just enough to catch a glimpse of the soldier's boots moving to the seat behind us. We kept our composure and our eyes shut. They were moving past us.

The soldier's machine gun bumped my head as he passed, but he didn't ask us to step out. Didn't he know he had hit my head with his machine gun?

It was as though we were frozen in time; we remained like statues with our eyes shut until they passed. And even then, we didn't move.

Hours seemed to pass until they reached the back of the bus, finished their search, walked back through the bus and exited the front doors.

"Are you okay?" I whispered to my son. He nodded slightly. "Stay still until the bus leaves." He complied.

In moments, the engine roared, the bus jerked, and we were on our way.

Nothing Short of Miraculous

What had just happened?

It was as though we were two ghosts, invisible in those two seats. Had God sent His angels to encompass us? Had He made us invisible? Were the soldiers blinded to our existence? We thanked God for answering our prayers.

We only knew He intervened in a supernatural way. He protected us from harm and perhaps even rescued us from the pit of a Bolivian prison—where my son could never have survived if we had been detained for any length of time. It was a miraculous rescue from unknown dangers.

When our bus finally turned off the bumpy, rough road into the mission school, we couldn't wait to exit and tell of God's miraculous protection.

What About Your Life?

The verse that had come to me in those long moments on the bus was, "In peace I will both lie down and sleep; for you alone, O LORD, make me dwell in safety" (Psalm 4:8). Amazingly, I felt peace knowing that He alone keeps us safe—sleeping or awake, with or without machine guns passing by our heads, and even while pretending to sleep.

Does God still do miracles today? Does He do things that seem impossible to us? Does He answer our prayers? You bet He does!

I'm sure He answers your prayers also. Maybe you haven't had machine guns pointed at your head, but possibly you've had sleepless nights with sick children or doctor's reports due in the morning or aging parents who need care. Whatever the circumstance (mountain) in your life, God can and will give you peace through it. Give it to Him and sleep!

Take Shape

- ❖ **Verse to Ponder:**

    "In peace I will both lie down and sleep; for you alone, O LORD, make me dwell in safety" (Psalm 4:8).

- ❖ **Question:**

    What keeps you from God's peace today?

- ❖ **Today's Exercise:**

    Sleeping may not seem like exercise, but it is. Because our muscles repair themselves when we sleep, they work out for us. So while we sleep, our body does rest exercises that regenerate us. Do you have trouble sleeping? Exercise by reminding yourself that you are sleeping in safety. This will pump up your soul's faith muscles so you are repaired and shaped spiritually, mentally, and physically by morning.

Sleeping peacefully in safety moves the mountain of fatigue.

God's Faithfulness
Feeling the Feathers

Have you ever seen God's wings or heard His feathers flutter? I have!

As we traveled from meeting to meeting and church to church one furlough, I shared this story whenever I had the opportunity. Maybe you've heard me tell it. If you have, I hope it made you realize how faithful our God is to meet our needs—even through condors.

Pain!

A few years ago, while we were at Rumi Rancho, my husband developed shingles. They healed in the usual amount of time, about three weeks. Not long after his recovery, though, he collapsed in severe pain. Not knowing whether he was having a heart attack or stroke, we rushed him to a clinic in our city. That excruciating pain lasted four hours. While the doctors gave him all the drugs possible without compromising his health in other ways, I doubted they were doing all they could to relieve this unbearable pain. At least we knew it wasn't a heart attack or stroke. (What we learned later was that the shingles had done severe damage to a nerve in Chuck's back. He would endure episodes like this for three years.)

That day, though, the pain began to subside a little. I couldn't believe the first words to slip through his lips as he looked up into my eyes: "I am so hungry for a pizza." Not what I expected to hear from a man who just came through this painful ordeal. How could I refuse such a request? We can't just call for takeout or pizza delivery, so I left him at the clinic and went home alone to make a pizza and fulfill this suffering man's wish.

At the Window

Eighteen years ago, while we were building our house, I insisted on having a big window in my kitchen. That may seem extravagant. But I spend many hours in that kitchen. Most of our food I make from scratch; I also teach teen girls baking and cooking classes as part of our mission. I love my kitchen window—even more now because of what I saw that day when I went home to make the love of my life a pizza.

As I whipped up the dough, I glanced out at that view. It's a rocky mountain, dry and brown most of the time, nevertheless a view of God's beautiful Andes Mountains. But this day, I didn't notice the mountain.

There, half way up sitting on a large, flat rock, sat two condors. Condors are the Bolivian national bird—but they're a rare site. They are on average four feet tall and have a wingspan of ten feet. Amazing creatures. Gigantic birds! We've lived in our house eighteen years and only once before had we seen a condor on this mountain. I rushed for the binoculars.

Fumbling, I placed them over my eyes. Condors, without a doubt. But that's not all. As I stood gazing with pure delight, something even more wonderful happened. Both birds, at precisely the same time, spread their wings and stood like statues. I could hardly breathe. God's beautiful creation reflecting all His glory. I stood in awe of these creatures created by an awesome God.

I knew those birds were there for me. I was alone that day. I knew people were praying for us, but no one had any idea what we were going through at that moment. Only God knew.

Not only was there one bird—a rare site in itself—but two birds—one for Chuck and one for me. So, I wasn't alone. God was with us both. I felt God's love around me—His feathers and His wings protecting me (Psalm 91:4). I looked at those birds standing there, wings spread, and knew God had me under His wings, as He did Chuck. I saw those wings, and I could faintly hear those feathers from my window. I saw God through condors, and I knew God would take care of us. I rested, snuggled under His wings, surrounded by His feathers of faithfulness.

God's Love Pictured

The depth of God's love is unimaginable. He shows us His love daily, even on occasion through condors. He covers us with His wings always. He shows Himself to us in the condor moments. Expect the condor moments. Watch for them. Don't miss them. Look. See God's wings and hear the gentle swish of His feathers.

Take Shape

- ❖ **Verse to Ponder:**

    "He will cover you with His feathers; you will take refuge under His wings. His faithfulness will be a protective shield" (Psalm 91:4 HCSB).

- ❖ **Question:**

    How have *you* experienced God's feathers?

- ❖ **Today's Exercise:**

    Mountain Climbing. It's necessary for mountain climbers to trust others with their lives and to trust each other as they climb up difficult mountains. They have to have the ability to face fears to be successful. We, too, climb mountains with God. The high ones and low ones shape our core faith as we go. And, we may occasionally experience condor moments that remind us to trust Him with our lives.

Climbing mountains with God moves the mountain of fear.

God's Teenagers
Meet the Parents

Wherever you call home, the teen years are a challenge for parents across most cultures. It wasn't so with our daughter. She always did what we asked and never gave us any major problems. With that in mind, you can imagine the scene when out of the blue she announced she had something important to tell us.

While we were serving on home staff at our mission headquarters, our daughter completed her high school senior year in the States. She grew into a beautiful, intelligent girl who turned eighteen and had never dated. She was involved in youth group at church and participated in the group activities. When she went out, she was always with the church group and never missed her curfew—a real gem of a daughter.

So, what was this *thing* she had to tell us? "I'm interested in a guy attending our youth group, and I want to date him." It wasn't an unreasonable request at her age, but the young man was a college student, four years older than Kristen. That concerned us a bit ... okay more than a bit. As I twirled a strand of hair falling across my brow, I glanced at my husband whose leg couldn't stop shaking. I knew we both needed time to digest this news and pray about our first meeting with this young *man* who wanted to date ou*r little girl.* We asked her to invite him over a few days later.

The Meeting!

The day arrived when she brought him home for the once-over. Poor guy, he appeared jittery—*as he should be*, I thought. But at the first sight of him, we understood the physical attraction. Tall, blonde, and huge blue eyes with an athletic body—what young girl wouldn't be attracted to him? Even more reason for our trepidation.

He sat on the floor playing with our dog—that immediately endeared him to us. Then he said something that made our mouths drop open. Sitting there in his shorts, all tan and handsome, he said,

"You may be wondering why I shave my legs."

That wasn't on our list of questions. We held our breath. What was he about to say?

"I'm on the university's cycling team, and shaving our legs helps us to gain speed." I'm sure our neighbors heard our sighs of relief.

After more conversation, our hearts softened toward this young man, and we approved the date.

As their relationship grew, he would cycle fifty miles from his university just to put a rose on our daughter's car parked outside her school. It was no surprise that in his senior year of college, he placed second in Florida's State Cyclists Championship.

Three years later, Chad and Kristen had a fairytale wedding in a park and have been married for twenty-two years. And, they have given us four adorable grandchildren. A happy ending and yes, Chad still shaves his legs and competes when time permits, but not often since he is a champion loving husband, father, and provider.

Shaved legs or not, we love him, and so does our daughter!

Take Shape

- ❖ **Verse to Ponder:**

    "Do not harden your hearts" (Psalm 95:8).

- ❖ **Question:**

    How can we be flexible to let go and still have input in our kids' lives?

- ❖ **Today's Exercise:**

    Cycling increases flexibility. Parents need flexibility, because every day new opportunities and obstacles arise. We can't be flexible with a hardened heart that won't change. God can change us and our children when our hearts are flexible and in tune with His heart. He desires to mold and shape our souls into His image.

Cycling with God through the many stages of life (including the dangerous curves of change) creates soft hearts within us and moves the mountain of inflexibility.

God's Protection
Valentine's Day Views

I've already told you some harrowing stories about our early mission days but let me backtrack a bit to our first day in Cochabamba, Bolivia.

Early on the morning of February 14, 1981, Valentine's Day, we touched down in Cochabamba. The view of the Andes Mountains from the plane's windows was breathtaking; they made the mountains of Pennsylvania look like molehills in comparison. Tucked into the mountainside and throughout the valley, we saw tiny mud huts—yet another reminder that we were in a foreign land.

A mission representative met us at the airport; then we climbed into the back of a truck and headed to the mission home. From there we got our first glimpses of Cochabamba, the second largest city in Bolivia. We felt the dust from dirt streets on our tired faces and bounced around when the driver swerved to miss an occasional pig or cow that darted in front of the truck. Our kids took it all in and loved every minute. I wondered why we were told Cochabamba was a big city. It looked more like a town in the movie "Butch Cassidy and the Sundance Kid." I had no idea this trip would seem like a "kiddie ride" compared to our next few weeks.

Fast-forward Excitement

Our bus trip to the mission school eight hours from the city confirmed that Bolivia had some of the most dangerous roads in the world with no guardrails between the roads and thousand-foot drop-offs. I can't forget to mention the drunk bus driver who drove as if he were in the Indy 500.

In our first month in Bolivia, Chuck was arrested in the marketplace for not having ID (then, too, his passport was in the capital city with our visa applications), a bomb went off down the street from the mission home where we were staying, and the president of the country threatened to cut the fingers off all missionaries. Before we were to be evacuated, there was a government overthrow, and the new president was more sympathetic to missionaries. Thankfully, we still have all our fingers.

Our life has continued to have the same thrills for thirty-seven years, and we have no plans of retirement, except a permanent retirement in a far better place with streets of gold.

Body Building

Why do we stay here? There can only be one answer: God put us in the ministry, and He has yet to call us out of it. Until He does, we are at work, *building His body*, His kingdom, in His strength.

For God so loved the world ...

We look forward to our first view of eternity, when, being shown through heaven maybe we'll have our first view of those we came to Bolivia to serve— those who accepted God's free gift, Jesus, and are now in that blissful place, in part because we made a few sacrifices to carry the gospel to them.

Take Shape

- ❖ **Verse to Ponder:**

    "For just as the body is one and has many members, and all the members of the body, though many, are one body, so it is with Christ" (1 Corinthians 12:12).

- ❖ **Question:**

    What ministries has God given you? What's your body-building task in the body of Christ? Are you apathetic in your relationships with other Christians or actively engaged in building the body of Christ?

- ❖ **Today's Exercise**:

    Body Building is the best sport when it comes to making your body proportionally shaped and fit. It helps all body parts work as one for the benefit of the whole.

    Body Building for God builds His Kingdom and fits us together so we all develop and prosper. We become concerned for the whole body of Christ. It shapes our souls into His image for His purpose.

Body Building with God moves the mountain of apathy.

God's Romance

Romantic Rides—The Cadillac Kiss

I married my *high school* sweetheart—he married his *childhood* sweetheart (me).

I hail from a tiny town nestled in the mountains of Pennsylvania. It was a whimsical time when the streets were safe, friends were many, and life was tranquil. Kids walked to school without the fear of predators. In this magical setting, at the tender age of nine, I had a constant annoyance on my walks to and from school—a boy—a pesky, persistent, presumptuous boy.

In my third-grade class this particular boy constantly annoyed me. Wherever I was, he somehow appeared. He insisted on walking home with me after school. He gave me gifts. Maybe in today's environment he could be tagged a stalker. Really, a third-grade, nerdy, short, skinny, and pesky boy doesn't fit the description of a stalker, but he most definitely fit the description of a pest. I was the goodie-two-shoes girl who towered above my classmates, even the boys. The contrast between my pest and me was one of a giant Amazon girl and an elf boy. Or, so I thought.

Worst Nightmare

This annoying relationship continued through our high school years. Reaching our senior year, we were the largest class in the history of our school. Because space was limited, lockers had to be shared. Can you imagine my horror when our teacher seated me behind my long-time pest and assigned us a locker together? Never in the school's history had a boy and girl shared a locker. There was no escape from my worst nightmare.

For weeks, I heard the same thing from this pest. Every day Chuck turned around in his seat and asked, "When will you go out with me?"

He always heard the same answer, "Never in your wildest dreams."

But he refused to give up. Finally, one day I caved. I couldn't hear that question one more time.

So, I made a deal. "I'll go out with you once if you promise that you will never ask me that question again."

He agreed!

I cringe thinking how cruel I was to a boy obviously enamored with me. I'm guessing you'd like to know how that date turned out. It had a surprising outcome—at least on my part. That night began two years of dating my worst enemy, and then a marriage that has lasted fifty years and counting.

You may wonder what happened to change my impressions of this young man. When my girlfriends asked why I was dating my worst enemy, I could only answer, "Because he is so nice." As I got to know Chuck, I realized what it was that I admired about my pest. He had a relationship with God, and his life reflected what he believed.

His Dad's Caddy

After six weeks of dating, I wondered when he might kiss me. One night after a school dance, he took me home in his dad's Cadillac. Shutting off the engine, he lingered for a moment before getting out to open my door as he always did. He leaned over and whispered, "What flavor is your lipstick?"

What kind of question was that?

Then he asked, "Can I taste your lipstick?" How sweet was that? He always conducted himself as a gentleman. Our first kiss was a Cadillac kiss!

Never Give Up

Valentine's Day for us is an anniversary of sorts. Chuck once gave me a bracelet on Valentine's Day when we were in grade school (when he was my worst enemy). As you know from the previous chapter, we also arrived in Bolivia the first time on Valentine's Day 1981.

The Bible says, "For my thoughts are not your thoughts, neither are your ways my ways, declares the LORD" (Isaiah 55:8).

As a child or teenager, I could never have imagined what God had planned for me. His plans certainly weren't my plans when I schemed to rid myself of the annoyance of this pesky boy. God's ways of joining together two people who were an unlikely match still amaze me today. But in His unfathomable plan, He transformed that pesky, nerdy boy into my Prince Charming.

This year on Valentine's Day, we'll celebrate thirty-seven years of ministry in Bolivia. We thank God for the love we share, the blessing of being together fifty years, and the ministry He called us to. I'm thankful that enamored, pesky boy never gave up until I said yes to him—and to God.

Take Shape

- **Verse to Ponder:**
  "For my thoughts are not your thoughts, neither are your ways my ways" (Isaiah 55:8).
- **Question:**
  Are you resisting God's thoughts today and missing what He wants you to do for Him?
- **Today's Exercise:**
  Horseback Riding is not just a sport for exercise benefits—although there are many— it's a partnership. If either the horse or the

rider resists, riding is impossible. Riding combines a cardiovascular workout with a rewarding mental challenge. Riders are typically a social crowd with a shared love of these majestic animals. It gives an opportunity to make friends with people you otherwise would never meet. Similarly, it wasn't my choice but God's to make a life-long friend of a boy with perseverance who annoyed me daily. It was God's plan for me to marry a man who shared my love of God. It's a partnership that will ride on through eternity—a partnership with God as He shapes our souls together for His purpose.

Horseback Riding is a partnership. And so is the Christian life. When we ride through life without resistance to God's will, the journey will be enjoyable. We must never quit riding (give up) until the horse enters the barn for the last time.

Riding with God, not against Him, moves the mountain of resistance.

God's Grandparents
Tips for Grandparenting from a Distance

In Rumi Rancho our daily goal is to show Christ's likeness, not ours, and to become more like Him daily. Our four grandchildren are just beginning this journey, and we have the challenge of planting seeds in their little hearts from a distance, helping them become like Him every chance we get.

One day, my granddaughter, Payton, saw another likeness in me when she came to visit. She was three when her whole family came to Bolivia one Christmas. It didn't take long for her to experience the frustration of learning a new language. Her big brother and sister were in a dual immersion school in U.S.A. and were able to communicate well in Spanish, their second language. They easily interacted with the Bolivian children, but not Payton. Understandable, since she was still learning her first language. With big blue eyes and white blonde hair, she immediately connected with me, her Grammie, in a unique way.

"Grammie!" she exclaimed one day, "I like you!"

Well, who wouldn't melt at that?

"Honey, I like you too," I replied, giving her a big hug and holding back the tears of joy.

"No!" She placed clenched fists on her hips. "I like you!" Each word came slowly and deliberately.

"I like you too, sweetie," was my patient reply.

Then with frustration in her little voice, she yanked her long ponytail over her head and pointed to my hair. "I *like* you!"

I finally got it. Her whitish hair and mine were the same color; she was identifying with me as her Grammie. In her mind, if she looked like me, she was *like* me. Her eyes twinkled in relief when she saw I finally understood.

I *Like* Jesus?

I was blessed that she saw our physical similarities, but could she see Jesus in me as well? I needed to know how I could impact my grandchildren's lives so they would be like Him. I think of Psalm 17:15, "As for me, I shall behold your face in righteousness; when I awake, I shall be satisfied with your likeness." We will be like Him someday, but what about now? Am I daily becoming more like Him?

God used a child to awaken me to the realization that I need to become more involved in my grandchildren's spiritual lives and to help them on their journey to become like Him.

Another Point of Contact

Ben, our oldest grandchild—quiet, reserved, and thoughtful—identified with us in a different way, through our children's ministry. All three visiting kids dug in and helped with our Christmas outreach for the needy children in the valley and in the mountain areas. Because they live far from civilization, they never receive Christmas gifts or have the opportunity to hear the gospel. It was our mission to bring them both.

Although our grandchildren were small

themselves, they saw the needs of the less fortunate and it changed their hearts. One day just before Christmas, as we drove home through villages where children lived in mud houses and played barefoot on dirt roads, Ben was noticing everything.

"Grammie? Can we give gifts to all the kids in every village?"

I was touched by the compassion of Jesus flowing through this young child.

All three grandkids joyfully helped wrap presents, bake cookies, and bag goodies for the big day. They even went with Grampie and took gifts and the Good News into remote areas. They were mini-missionaries for Jesus. They soon connected with our vision, and a heart for missions was planted. Kayla, our oldest granddaughter, indicated her desire to come back and work with us "forever" helping needy children and telling them about Jesus.

Soon it was time for our grandchildren to return home. It was hard to see our time together end, knowing there would be years between our next visit. The house was suddenly sad and empty, and most on my heart was how could I stay in touch and influence their lives for Jesus from Bolivia. Instead of "I like you, Grammie," from Payton I longed to hear, "I like Jesus." I long to hear that she's loving Him, liking Him, becoming like Him more each day, with my help.

Tell the Story

It was then that God gave me an idea to write stories for them about the animals they had come to know and love while visiting us. Each story had a tie-in to a biblical principle. It was a way for me to connect with them and teach them about God from a distance.

As they grew and changed, I asked God for new ways to connect to them—to reach their world. In answer to my prayers, God reminded me of my love for writing for children and of the creative opportunities today's technologies offer.

So, I started writing children's devotions and drawing my grandchildren into the writing circle with me. I sent them to websites to read devotionals—

sometimes they were mine. They learned what I was writing about, and it got them in the Word. This plan is motivating them and giving them a desire to be in God's Word.

No matter what ideas God gives me, I want to stay available for Him to use me in their lives.

We now have another grandson, Baden. He keeps me motivated to write for little ones. When my *Really Rare Rabbits* series was published, I sent him a copy each time a new book released. Sometimes he asks the mailman if there is another book from his Grammie in the mail. Oh, my heart!

So You Never Forget ...

When Kayla was five, she spoke twelve words to me that are forever etched in my heart. She bent down and picked a flower as we were saying goodbye before our return to Bolivia that year. "Here Grammie, this is for you, so you will never forget me." I made a promise never to forget her (or her family) and to always be in touch regardless of the miles between us.

Little Payton once made a profound statement when her mom told her we were going bowling in Bolivia. She gave her mom a puzzled look and said, "You mean they can do that in their world?" Whether we live nearby or far away, all grandparents live in a different world from their grandchildren in some way. It's up to us to find ways to connect those different worlds so our grandchildren can learn from our example what Jesus is really like.

Payton began swimming when she was four and won medal after medal. Now, she is fourteen and other swimmers in her age group want to emulate her ability and win medals too. In her swim world, she is an example of determination and dedication to her sport that drives others to reach their goals, too. Shouldn't our example as Christians drive others to follow Christ and reach for a life dedicated to Him in our world?

I know it will be a continuing journey, trusting God for new ideas and plans as my grandchildren grow into adults; but it's a journey I don't want to miss. When I look at those replicas of us and see

Jesus shining through, two worlds melt into one.

We are pressing to that day when we awake, finally, with His likeness, in His new world, where we will all be like Him forever, our journey over with no more distance between us. We'll all say, "I like Jesus," and we will actually *be* like Him.

Take Shape

- ❖ **Verse to Ponder:**
    "As for me, I shall behold your face in righteousness; when I awake, I shall be satisfied with your likeness" (Psalm 17:15).
- ❖ **Question**:
    How do you look like Jesus?
- ❖ **Today's Exercise:**
    Swimming is said to turn back the clock. Who doesn't want to look younger? Experts tell us that swimming puts us in a good mood. But isn't it better to want to look like Jesus and have a Jesus mood no matter our age? When we smile our genuine joy makes us look more like Jesus.

Swimming through life with determination and dedication to God—despite the waves of trials and moods—will make us look like Jesus, shaped to glorify Him. The joy of the Lord will shine through us, and we will encourage others to "swim" with God.

Swimming *with* God's current, not against it, moves the mountain of discouragement.

God's Grandmothers
In My Grandmother's Eyes

She was my grandmother, but more than that she was my "Mom." What a unique and wonderful combination! She was a remarkable lady who rescued a motherless, eight-month-old baby girl—me.

This self-sacrificing grandmother stepped up to the challenge of caring for me, a helpless baby, when my mother abandoned my dad and me to start a new life thousands of miles away. The divorce devastated my dad, and I doubt he ever got over the pain of losing the love of his life. He relinquished the care of his baby to his mother, while he tried to begin a new life for himself; but he never seemed to find happiness to displace the hurt in his heart.

My grandmother never thought twice about caring for me, even though she was nearly fifty years old. She swooped me up to become my protector and provider; I was safe under her wings. She nurtured and loved me with a mother's love, comparing to nothing else except a grandma's love; I had them both rolled into one. I became her little princess; she curled my hair every day and dressed me royally. I looked like the Shirley Temple of our small town.

Life was glorious; my clothes were delivered to my closet as though from a laundry service, my bed was made by my fairy godmother, and meals were always on time and fit for a princess. This virtuous woman never had an unkind word to say about anyone, and she always praised my real mother. *That* must say something about the lady; she praised the daughter-in-law who disappeared, leaving her baby.

Standard of Perfection

We grandmothers all want to lavish our grandchildren with love. We don't necessarily want the responsibility of disciplinarian; my grandmother didn't want that role either. In fact, I enjoyed the benefits of that part of the union. I was the princess of the house, never required to do chores. My grandmother did all the work, while I got all the blessings.

She had a housekeeper once a week, but since her requirements for cleanliness far exceeded other peoples' standards, she would clean her house before the cleaning lady arrived. No one could enter her doors unless the house was spotless, not even the cleaning lady.

That is probably the reason I am inclined to be a perfectionist; but God gave me the husband who understands my eccentricities—built into me after years of being a childhood princess.

I believe that God, in a miraculous way through my anything-but-normal childhood, used the years with my grandmother to mold me into His servant, ready to serve Him in a foreign land. He gave both my husband and me a love for children and, in particular, a heart for Bolivia's children.

Meet Your Mother

I will always be grateful for my grandma's influence that led me to a life of helping children. She is the reason I grew up with no animosity toward my biological mother (whom I met when I was twenty-three, beside the casket of her mother, my maternal grandmother). We formed a friendship and love for each other, and we keep in touch now. People often ask what that meeting was like emotionally. I respond by saying, "If you were to meet a stranger today what would be your emotional response?"

That's how it was, no emotion for me, and surprisingly I had no desire to hug this lady I resembled in many ways. However, the emotional roller coaster ride leading to the encounter was another story. Planning for the event made me more nervous than the actual meeting. We had a two-year old son, her grandson. How would I choose to handle that? If this woman never wanted to see her daughter in all those years, why would she want to see her grandson? Would I take him with me or wait for her to ask to see him? I chose to let her request the meeting, which she eventually did.

The emotions were in high gear as I entered the funeral home where my mother's mother was being viewed; my husband was by my side. It was ironic that my maternal grandmother had always wanted the two of us to meet, and now her body lay in a casket close to the scene where the meeting would finally take place.

Princess Peggy finally met her real mother; but the example I had daily growing up was still the one I desired to emulate every day of my life. My grandmother may not have been my biological mother, but she was my real mother in every sense of the word. She worked hard, especially for me, and gave generously of all she had. She served others always.

By Example

When I married Chuck, I didn't know much about cooking or cleaning, but I knew I wanted to be like the woman I loved and admired. I wanted to have a clean house, be a fantastic cook, and serve others as she did daily. Maybe Grandma didn't make me do things a wife, mother, or grandmother would do, but better yet, she showed me how to be that woman by her example. I learned those things almost by osmosis. After I was married, I spent hours watching and learning from her as she continued working well into her eighties, serving others and cooking for the family restaurant.

Through my childhood Grandma worked in the restaurant, making her special dishes and overseeing the business. Every time she left our beautiful house, I worried she wouldn't come back because of an accident. I wanted to go everywhere with her so I could protect her from harm. Psychologists would say I feared being abandoned again, there may be some truth in that. But contrary to what any mental health professional would say, I never feared being abandoned by my grandmother. My greatest fear was that through uncontrollable circumstances, not of her choosing, she would be taken out of my life. I knew she would never leave me willingly. My biggest struggle leaving home to serve in Bolivia was leaving her behind. She's in heaven now, and I miss her; but she didn't leave me, she is in my heart forever.

Some may think it was a tragic childhood, but I would disagree because I felt blessed. Romans 8:28 tells us that all things work together for good. My life is proof that no matter what circumstances we encounter, God can use them to fulfill His will and His purpose in our lives.

I am blessed to have found my purpose and experience the joy of serving God. My Grandma/Mom was used of God to raise a child who would help build His kingdom in a foreign land. She is probably up there shining the streets of gold on her hands and knees right now, whether they need polishing or not.

I thank God for putting me in her arms as a baby, and for all she did to make my life happy and blessed. I strive every day to serve Jesus with all my heart; I got a glimpse of who He was through her life of service.

Take Shape

❖ **Verse to Ponder:**
   "Give her of the fruit of her hands, and let her works praise her in the gates" (Proverbs 31:31).

❖ Question:

How will you influence your grandchildren or other people's grandchildren? Will you be honored and praised for your work like my grandmother deserves to be honored?

❖ Today's Exercise:

Gardening. According to Mayo Clinic, gardening can be restoring. It gives you something to nourish and cultivate. It also gives back by producing flowers, vegetables, and fruit to nourish your body. I represent my grandmother's garden. Restored in spirit and health and nourished by her loving-care, I thrived and bloomed—and now am able to give back to the Master Gardener by serving Him in His garden and bearing eternal fruit for Him.

Gardening together with God allows Him to plant, cultivate, and shape our souls so we grow up from His soil of love—beautiful inside and out as we bloom daily for Him.

Gardening with God moves the mountain of weeds that hinder us from blooming.

God's Will

Spring Cleaning Your Soul

We'd served on the mission field sixteen years when bizarre circumstances threatened to jolt us out of our ministry. The mission organization under which we served experienced radical changes. Almost overnight we lost half our support because of those changes. The looming problems caused some supporters and friends to wonder if God wanted us to return to the field. Even so, we believed God wanted us back in Bolivia. It was a time when I wondered if I'd lose all hope in the face of a furious storm that I thought would never pass.

Perhaps you've had experiences that led you to a similar emotional state. I suppose that within our Christian bubble, we expect to be protected from life's storms. We assume God will keep us from harm and hurting hearts. But even though we are new creatures in Christ, we live in a fallen world. Its problems creep into our churches, Christian organizations, and our daily encounters with Christian brothers and sisters. People hurt us—even churches, pastors, leaders, and yes, even our families. Problems infiltrate our insulated world and our personal mission fields.

I was convinced nothing good could come from this bursting of my Christian bubble. I didn't have to pray to know that. So I didn't bother. The situation was so complicated, I didn't believe God could fix it or change it—and He didn't. Instead, I see from my vantage point today that through it, He changed me.

During this harrowing season, I went from a person who always smiled to a person who couldn't stop crying. When I did make a feeble attempt to pray, I was certain my prayers hit the ceiling and bounced back.

The Dark Place

During our months of transition, I had no idea I was plummeting to a dark place, but others feared it was inevitable. My husband became concerned about my daily sadness. The more I tried to fix our situation, the worse it became. I felt as though God had abandoned me. Of course, He hadn't, nor had our most loyal supporters and friends. They believed God's promise, "Never will I leave you; never will I forsake you" (Hebrews 13:5 NIV). If only I could believe as they did. They knew God had a plan and so did my husband. I, however, couldn't see beyond my broken heart. At that point Chuck suggested I take a thousand-mile trip to visit my dear friend for a week. He thought it might help me begin healing and give me time to pray and be with friends who cared.

So, what did it take to jolt me back to God—to trust Him no matter what? It took the right words at the right time. Proverbs 15:23 says, "A man takes joy in giving an answer, and a timely word—how good that is!" I did fly across the country to see my friend. Reluctantly, I boarded the plane. Thankful for a window seat, I stared at the heavens for hours. My hands wrenching and tears pouring over my face, I felt close to God there in the clouds. It had been a long time since I'd felt His presence.

Believing, Trusting Prayer

My friend welcomed me into her home. After a few days of good food, rest, and praying together, she sat me down for a talk. I knew I didn't want to hear what she had to say. I fidgeted when she sat on the edge of the bed, squeezed my sweaty hand, and began to speak her mind.

"You are not the person I've known for so long." Now that stung! Then again, she was right. I wasn't. What she couldn't bring herself to say was, "Don't you believe Jesus' words?"

John 14:13 says, "And I will do whatever you ask in my name, so that the Son may bring glory to the Father" (NIV). I'd stopped praying or asking. I feared His answer would not be the answer I wanted. I'd left Jesus out of the problems, but He hadn't abandoned me. I knew He was sitting on that bed with us. I knew what I had to do. I prayed. And for the first time in ages, I prayed believing He would answer. I confessed my disbelief and gave my life to God—again. Then, I asked for *His* will, not mine. If He wanted Chuck and me in Bolivia, that's where we'd be. If not, I trusted Him for our future. My friends were relieved to see me smile. God answered their prayers.

What happened next could only be explained as God's answer to prayer. It had been a year since we'd begun raising support, praying for God's will about our return to the mission field. We'd shared our ministry in many churches and groups, but we didn't have the funds needed to return to our ministry. Was that His answer to our prayers?

What Happened Next ...

We decided to draft a newsletter. Only God knew our request, "If it's Your will we return to the field, show us by supplying the support we need in the next few weeks from this letter. If not, we'll know You want us to stay in the States." Would it be the last newsletter we'd write as missionaries or the first one on our way back to Bolivia? We dropped 350 newsletters in the mail. It had no mention of our prayer for support. Our answer had to come from God and not from a plea for funds.

What happened next lifted me immeasurably. God's family embraced us with His love and encouraged us to head back to Bolivia. Calls came daily for new meetings. Churches where we had spoken months before wrote to tell us they had added us to their budget. Within weeks, we had the necessary support; within months, we were back in Bolivia. God provided and had more wonderful plans in store for our future.

Take Shape

- **Verse to Ponder:**

    "If we confess our sin, He is faithful and righteous to forgive us our sins and to cleanse us from all unrighteousness" (1 John 1:9 HCSB).

- **Question:**

    Do you confess your sin and allow God to spring clean your soul?

- **Today's Exercise:**

    Spring Cleaning. When spring begins to show its sunny face, I plan my deep-cleaning itinerary. It's time to take out the rubber gloves, buy special cleaners (I love Murphy's Oil Soap), and get ready to exercise my whole-body muscles. Some days, I overdo the scrubbing and pay the price with legs that limp to the recliner in the evening and arms that refuse to lift a fork at dinnertime. When we deep clean, we prevent gross dirt build up through hard work. When we finish, our houses sparkle and smell clean.

Likewise, when we spring clean our souls, God wipes away the crud that prevents us from following God. The hard-to-reach places in our souls shine again. It causes us to dig down to the nooks and crannies of disobedience we tend to ignore and the faults we cover up.

After confessing our sin, we can love and serve one another with new radiance—we shine His light, bright and clean. Many souls' eternal lives depend on our obedience here. Actually, like weekly house cleaning, cleaning our souls with daily confession makes spring cleaning easier.

Spring cleaning with God cleanses our soul with confession and moves the mountain of built-up sin and disobedience.

God's Plans
Plans That Prosper

About two years after the events that led to our return to Bolivia, we found ourselves on the threshold of another major change. What were God's plans for our ministry? We'd been through rough waters for a few years, but now there was excitement, not sadness, in the uncertainty as we looked for guidance.

Our seven years of work in a rural village in Bolivia was showing fruit. The church was established, and our youth ministry grew beyond expectations. God led us to begin classes to teach practical skills and Bible to the youth in the area, encouraging more young people to attend church. The classes began in a church leader's mud house, a place with no bathrooms or running water, typical of village living conditions.

Our travel from the city five times a week was an hour's drive over rough terrain. On one trip, we were chatting along and began discussing a furlough for the future. We'd been back on the field two years and didn't know how we'd ever leave the ministry for a long furlough the following year. It seemed wise to take a short furlough that summer for only two months. If we were gone any longer, we feared the work we had accomplished might regress.

The moon wasn't shining, and there were no streetlights that night as we bumped along. Electricity hadn't reached the area yet, but I think our faces illuminated from God's blessings of our growing ministry. The conversation was pleasant until my husband blurted out a proposition I had never considered and honestly didn't want to discuss. "I think the Lord wants us to move out here. We could do so much more ministry if we didn't have to spend so much time traveling."

Words every missionary wife wants to hear, right? We'd have to uproot and move from the conveniences of the city to the boonies and live in a mud hut, no phones or electricity—all those things we think we can't live without. Besides, we'd need to buy land and build a house, and we didn't have a penny for that! What was Chuck thinking? But what if they were God's thoughts, guiding us to His place of future ministry? I had to consider that.

Without hesitation, I blurted, "If God wants us to move out here then He's going to have to make it *very* clear." I was comfy, but I knew I wouldn't be content staying still when God wanted us to pack our bags. Still, I hoped this was just a passing whim of my husband and not a redirection from God.

Clear Direction

We took the two-month furlough and shared with our supporters all God was doing in the village and how He seemed to be leading us to live in the area of our ministry. Never had we seen such an outpouring of gifts as we saw during those months. Donations ranged from computers and printers for teaching kids who had no opportunity to learn these skills, to a quad for getting around the remote villages, and of course, prayers and love from God's people. Funds poured into our office for shipping the supplies and even a down payment to buy land and build. It was *very* clear what God wanted us to do next. He answered our prayers—again.

Today, almost two decades later, we look around and see God's provision everywhere. He provided a brick (not mud) house, a chapel, classroom buildings, electricity, and phones, and even running water. We have a ministry teaching practical skills to children while reaching them for Christ. More than 3,000 kids have passed through our doors (and more through our churches) and heard about Jesus. They now can pray in Jesus' Name. Both of our Bolivian churches are growing and training disciples, and God led us to start a new mission. To God be the glory!

When the Plan Is God's

Yes, God had a plan. It wasn't my plan, but His. I learned through prayer that even when we are sinking in the storm, God is with us, and He is in control. God is always working for our good, no matter what storms we face—and He always has a plan. He answers prayers.

There is a cross-stitch on my office wall that

says, *God gives the very best to those who leave the choice to Him—Jim Elliot.* I can attest to the truth of that statement. God brought me through the storm and gave me the best when I finally left the choice to Him. He put me where He wanted me to be: in a special place, in His perfect time, and for His eternal purpose.

When the storms come again (and I know they will), I want to plant my feet on the solid ground of prayer, and never doubt Him. I want to seek His plans, the only plans that ultimately prosper.

Take Shape

- ❖ **Verse to Ponder**:
    "For I know the plans I have for you," declares the Lord, "plans to prosper you and not harm you, plans to give you a future and a hope" (Jeremiah 29:11).
- ❖ **Question:**
    Are you seeking God's plans so you will prosper? Will you flex your faith muscles daily and believe His plans are best?

❖ **Today's Exercise**:

Rowing is helpful both for beginners and exercise gurus. Its benefit is that you can begin with no muscles and build as you go. You can begin with God like that, too. Decide to row with God whether you are a baby Christian or a mature Christian. And if you haven't yet believed God's message, you can decide today to accept His free gift of salvation through His Son. You can start rowing with Him this instant. And, when you're in the boat and the storms come, keep rowing. God will build your faith and shape your soul muscles as you go. Just start believing His plans are best. Don't waver. He has a plan for you, and He'll never let you sink.

Rowing with God moves the mountain of wavering and keeps your life afloat.

God's Direction
God's Travel Tips: Paths to Divine Direction

Imagine standing in my front yard, on the property God provided for us. You see cactus plants, and feel a prick when your arm accidentally brushes one. You're wrapped in a warm breeze, but the mountaintops of the Andes above are covered with snow—you shiver. People live in those mountains without basic necessities of life. Their mud huts with dirt floors and no windows barely give them shelter.

It is not uncommon for people today to migrate either cross-country or around the world. In Bolivia, migration is becoming a necessary part of life. The mountainous areas don't have water, electricity or sufficient, nutritious food supplies. So many come down from the mountains into the larger communities below. Those who do often experience culture shock. But probably few experience as much as the migrator I'd like to introduce to you today.

Meet Young Juan

The migration begins in a place far from civilization, where we meet a migrator who made a journey, not just from a rural village to a bustling city, but from a life of isolation to a life of service to the King of kings. Imagine the culture shock of a young man who had lived in a mud hut and spoken only Quechua, until he was thrust into a modern Spanish-speaking culture of a Bolivian city. As if that weren't enough, he entered a third culture—the culture of a foreign country while living with us, missionaries from the United States.

Here's how Juan describes the place where he was born and the circumstances of his childhood. "I was born in the small village of Umamarca, high in the Andes Mountains of Bolivia. I lived without electricity and the basic needs that we live with today. I walked a mile every day for water from a spring on a hillside and ate salty dried meat and potatoes most days. When I was two years old, my mother had an accident. She was hiking up a hill to separate two fighting cows and fell, causing the premature birth of my sister. They both died that day."

Two years later, Juan's dad also had an accident. A mud wall collapsed on him, and he was buried for two hours before being rescued. Afterward, he was partially paralyzed. The responsibility of caring for his dad fell on four-year-old Juan. He worked for an aunt and uncle in their potato fields and got paid with discarded potatoes—it was all they had to eat. After a few years, Juan's dad was able to walk with the aid of crutches and frequently hobbled down the mountain with Juan to green pastures where their sheep grazed. Juan's hikes down the mountain became slow strolls with his dad at his side.

Juan told me, "On one such journey, we wandered into a small church—actually, a small mud building. We heard singing and went inside. For the first time, we heard the gospel preached and accepted the Lord." Then Juan told me about the first time he saw a puppet presentation at age eight. "I thought there were tiny people inside the puppets."

Culture shock.

Juan Learns to Trust God

When Juan was fourteen, he decided to move his dad and stepmother to the Cochabamba valley where they could seek medical help and a better life. Their only income on the mountain had been planting and selling potatoes, but they were barely able to buy food with the profits. How could they make the journey, and how could Juan know if he would find a job and a place to live? As missionaries we've come to know the truth of the Proverbs 3:5-6 promise: "Trust the Lord ... and He will direct your path." But how could Juan trust God? How could he even know the God who directs our steps?

Yet Juan was sure God was moving them to the city. They gathered their few belongings and got into the back of a potato truck. It was Juan's first time in a vehicle. "Arriving in the city, we stayed in a garage where other people from the mountain stayed when they visited to sell potatoes. The next day, I sat in the town plaza waiting for a job offer. I was offered a job to guard a house and harvest potatoes in a nearby village. When the potatoes were harvested, I looked for another job but couldn't find one.

I returned to the mountain, married, and later returned to the city with my wife and baby. A year had passed, and jobs were hard to find. We moved in with my dad and stepmother while I continued to look for work. While out walking to inquire about a job, I passed a house being built. The missionary who was building saw me and asked if I needed a job. I became a construction worker there by day and a watchman by night. The pay was more than I ever dreamed—of course, I was doing two jobs, so double the pay."

Twenty Years of Growing in Christ

Chuck and I were the missionaries who hired Juan. Often Chuck would tell Juan how God brought him to our door the exact day we needed someone to guard the construction equipment. That was almost twenty years ago. Juan eventually taught our computer classes, became a leader in our church, and helped us in all aspects of our ministry.

A young boy trusted God and migrated from the isolated mountains of Bolivia to a place where God used him mightily for His Kingdom. Juan and his family lived on our property with their two children in a small house we built for them. He left a place where he didn't have basic human needs and found God able to provide his every need. He trusted God's travel tips, and God led him to his divine destination. In Juan's words, (as it says in Ephesians 3:20), "I am abundantly blessed above all I could have asked or thought."

Take Shape

- **Verse to Ponder:**

    "You are blessed when you stay on course, walking [hiking] steadily on the road revealed one step at a time by God. You're blessed when you follow His directions, doing your best to find Him. That's right—you don't go off on your own; you walk [hike] straight along the road He set. You, God, prescribed the right way to live; now you expect us to live it. Oh, that my steps might be steady, keeping to the course you set; then I'd never have any regrets in comparing my life with your counsel. I thank you for speaking straight from your heart; I learn the pattern of your righteous ways. I'm going to do what you tell me to do; don't ever walk [hike] off and leave me" (Psalm 119:1-8 MSG).

❖ **Question:**

Will you "hike" with God to see and hear the things He has waiting for you and be sensitive to His leading daily? Are you sensitive to those around you who may need you to hike with them on their journey?

❖ **Today's Exercise:**

Hiking creates awareness in our eyes and ears and the rest of our senses. It also nourishes our imagination. Enjoying nature as we hike increases our awareness of God's presence. It shapes our soul's senses and opens our hearts to the needs of others.

Hiking with God moves the mountain of insensitivity.

God's Presence
A Deserted Place

Life seems to be on fast-forward for everyone, and I'm no exception. But God is working in our ministry and our lives in marvelous ways, and we are seeing many come to know the Lord, through our churches and Rumi Rancho.

When life gets so busy, it's easy not to spend time with the One who gives us all those blessings. I asked the Lord daily for so many things—understanding of all I'm learning, health to do it all, and provision for our ministry and us—along with prayers for family, friends, and safety. And, I tell the Lord I want to spend more time with Him—but sometimes I put Him on hold, so to speak. Yes, I have devotions, and yes, I meditate on Scripture, but when do I block out everything so I can hear His voice?

When I ask, God gives me that time. Not long ago, I hadn't made focused time for Him, so He arranged a quiet place to be with Him. It was as if He said to Chuck and me, "Come away to a deserted place all by yourselves and rest a while" (Mark 6:31 NRSV).

Searching While the Internet Is Down

After waiting days, our Internet server's tech guy finally arrived to find and fix the problem we were having with our speed. To do the fix, though, the tech guy had to cut our service. After pleading with God that He hurry those men along so I could get to the things I had to do, I heard Him say, "Come with Me." I closed my computer and opened my Bible. I began reading in Psalms where I had stopped the day before, "Praise be to the Lord my Rock, who trains my hands for war, my fingers for battle" (Psalm 144:1 NIV).

I could relate to the Psalmist. Any time we are giving God's Word out, we engage in that battle, and it is nothing short of war. The enemy will do anything to keep God's Word from spreading. Now that I write to get God's Word out, I feel that opposition even more. Never before did I encounter so many internet problems that can't seem to be resolved. And, some days I feel like my head is going to explode from all the new things I am putting into it.

Refreshed by His Presence

After spending time in God's Word that day of frustration without internet, I felt less uptight with the long delay in restoring the service. Instead, I took a walk with God up the mountain behind our house. There were no camels there in my desert, only two ponies and what seemed like thousands of birds singing praises to God—a little bit of heaven, a little time with my Creator.

I didn't have to travel to an exotic, faraway place to get away from it all (I already live in one), I just needed to be refreshed by His presence. I know God will teach me what I need to know so I can accomplish the work He has for me. He is training my hands and my fingers to write for Him. He told me that when I walked with Him.

Take Shape

- ❖ **Verse to Ponder:**

    "You ... are my servant, serving on my side. I've picked you. I haven't dropped you. Don't panic. I'm with you. There's no need to fear for I'm your God. I'll give you strength. I'll help you. I'll hold you steady, keep a firm grip on you" (Isaiah 41:9-10 MSG).

- ❖ **Question:**

    What talent is God developing in you for His ministry and His glory? Will you come away with Him regularly to be refreshed and continue to grow and learn of His ways? Only He gives us skills and talents and makes us competent. He equips us when we spend time in His presence.

- ❖ **Today's Exercise:**

    Grip Exercises increase dexterity in the fingers. They strengthen joints and expand capacity to lift weight. God's got a grip on us and gives us strength to rise above the weight of our burdens to accomplish His purpose. He trains our fingers and minds so we win the battles of life and ultimately prevail with Him in the war.

Grip God's hand, enter His presence, feel His hand grip yours, and allow Him to train you and move the mountain of incompetency.

God's Healing
Freaky Face

When we arrived in Bolivia we were asked to work at the school for missionary children. A few days later and after much prayer, we accepted the challenge and headed to our destination. As the early morning fog lifted, we boarded the small mission plane and flew to the school eight hours from the city. We landed with a thump on the short mountaintop airstrip. Cacti and desert terrain surrounded us. We realized this remote situation would isolate us from the outside world. But because God led us to this place, we willingly made it our home for five years. Our children enjoyed every scary detail of the adventure.

Chuck settled into the role of business manager of the mission station. My role was dorm parent for twenty-seven teenaged girls and librarian. After a four-month initiation into missionary work, the school year ended and our crash course in Spanish began.

Lesson in Something Other Than Spanish

Not only was I beginning Spanish study, but I also started having symptoms of a mysterious illness. Each morning, I awoke with a different part of my face swollen. At first, the mission doctor (eight hours away) thought it was caused by insect bites from a *vinchuca*, a parasite insect that carries disease. We fumigated the dorm, but I had no relief.

We finally decided it was an allergy, and we tried to find the cause. Nothing changed, and my face became distorted from the swelling—I called it a freaky sight. I cringed when I looked at myself; putting on make-up only enhanced the grotesque reflection in the mirror. I was barely recognizable but continued to go to class regardless of my appearance.

Five months after arriving in Bolivia, I went to my regular Spanish class. But that day was different—anything but regular; during class, my nose began to run. Chuck looked over and handed me a Kleenex, but I couldn't reach for it.

I was paralyzed. Chuck realized something was wrong and grabbed me. Other missionary students helped him lower me to the floor. I could see and hear, but I couldn't move.

Chuck wrapped me in a blanket and with help from others, carried me to the school clinic. I lost my sight. I knew my husband was on my right side and the nurse on the left and two friends flanked my body.

Just then I saw bright lights. "I think I'm dying." I felt calm and drifted into unconsciousness.

When I awakened, I was in the school clinic alive, but paralyzed. My head, packed in ice to reduce the swelling in my brain, was pounding and cold. I shivered. Chuck was holding my hand, and his tired eyes revealed his concern.

Diagnosis: Leave the Field

As the swelling in my brain subsided, the movement of my body returned, first one side, then the other. Two days later, the mission plane transported me to a city hospital.

At the hospital, they injected me with steroids

and put me on a strict diet. I improved, but the diagnosis wasn't what we wanted to hear. They said I was allergic to something in the area of the school. We would have to leave the area, and possibly Bolivia.

The doctors warned I would die if we stayed at the school. Would we try to work in another part of Bolivia only to find I had the same problem there or return to the United States? We loved our ministry. Why would God have prepared us, and provided for us to be in Bolivia, just to have us return home after six months?

A Second Opinion—God's

We asked the leaders of the mission to pray over me and trusted God to heal me. They came and prayed. I slept peacefully that night knowing I was in God's hands.

The next morning, I faced another decision. What did I do next? I had taken a step of faith, now I had to act on it. I asked God to give me the faith to trust and act.

I stopped the injections and the restrictive diet. My taste buds were alive again, everything that touched my tongue was delicious. My face returned to its normal size and image within a week.

I was healed. A few weeks passed, and still I had no sign of the swelling in my face. On Tuesday nights, we gathered for staff meetings, but this Tuesday night, something eerie happened. During our meeting, my lip started to swell as it had in the previous months—first the lip then my whole face. Everyone at the school knew of my healing, but some still questioned if I shouldn't leave the area for my safety. As my face swelled more that night, my husband rose out of his chair and asked for prayer. Not just any prayer but prayer that we'd resist the devil, and claim God's healing—again. Within minutes, the swelling disappeared. Usually, the swelling only subsided with cortisone and required hours for my face to return to normal. Did I believe God had healed me? Yes! Did others see God's hand as we did and believe also? Yes!

Those mysterious allergies never returned. Thirty

years later, I'm still alive and living in Bolivia. My freaky face is gone, but the memory of a miracle is forever with me. Yes, God heals in many miraculous ways—He even heals a freaky face.

Take Shape

- **Verse to Ponder:**

    "Therefore, submit to God. But resist the Devil, and he will flee from you" (James 4:7 HCSB).

- **Question:**

    Do you give up easily or do you resist the devil and defeat him?

- **Today's Exercise:**

    Resistance Training increases stamina. As you grow stronger, you don't tire as easily. The more weight you bear, the more you resist giving up. Likewise, the more we resist the devil, the more our soul muscles strengthen and our faith increases. Each victory over sin builds our faith. We resist the temptation to give up, and we don't give in to the devil.

Acts 20:24 says, "However, I consider my life worth nothing to me, if only I may finish the race and complete the task the Lord Jesus has given me."

Resistance Training with God moves the mountain of defeat—resist the devil, gain strength, and complete your task for the Lord—never defeated.

God's Friends
Why We Need Underwear Friends

Underwear. We all wear it and need it, I'm guessing. You can find it in many varieties: large, small, colored or white, old, new, fancy, and simple. Underwear is the closest thing to us; just like underwear friends. Underwear friends knit us together when the wedgies of life cause us to come apart at the seams.

Poops is my chief underwear friend. You heard me right. That's her real nickname! Who could make that up? Poops began her underwear ministry thirty years ago when I left for Bolivia and has bought me underwear ever since. She is an experienced and proficient shopper and knows how to buy underwear that is pretty, comfy, and never gives you a wedgie. Poops is like that too, always pretty, comfy to be around, and never gets her undies in a bundle—a faithful friend.

Poops has bought me everything from *Cuddl*

Duds® (to keep me warm), to *Spandex* (to gird me up). When I shared with her that a friend had deeply hurt me, she had words of wisdom for me. "We are all imperfect. When a friend gives you a wedgie forgive her, but first pluck out your own wedgie before attempting to pluck out your sister's."

Yikes, how many wedgies have I allowed to creep up on my friends?

Friends Who Bless and Encourage

Poops isn't my only underwear friend. Friends like Connie Lou who sewed my underwear and gave me a needling when I needed it. A friend who spoke the truth in love, even though it pinched a bit, but snapped me back to reality when I was down.

Then there's Cookie, who lets me sit on her couch and vent. And Lois, who washed and line dried my laundry—underwear included—when I didn't have the time. (Occasionally, on our furloughs, we're so busy traveling that I carry our dirty laundry with me.) I have friends who lift the burdens, like a girdle. Their washers cleanse the dirt while we visit, and our time together washes away the stress.

They do all sorts of things for us, those underwear friends. They are churches, ladies' groups, and Sunday school classes filled with people who love us and give us a sense of home. If you're supporters of our ministry, you know them: those who manage the home office, supporters and prayer partners; they invite you to meals or take you shopping, and write you emails. They sit and listen for hours to our stories and allow us to fall asleep on their couches.

They've given us precious memories of game nights, laughing into the wee hours, and Christmas in October. When we need a ride to the airport or hospital, they are ready and they open their homes so we have a place to lay our heads. They are Jesus on earth for us, our blessings of unconditional love.

Who Are Your Underwear Friends?

Do you have underwear friends? We all need them, because we are all in the battle. In the Women of Faith book, *Friendship: Cultivating Relationships*

That Enrich Our Lives, Margaret Feinberg writes that friends are like treasures: "The best kinds of friends in life are those who love us despite our wrinkles and warts. They have a knack for drawing the best out of us and challenging us to grow into all we were meant to be in our journey of life and faith."

My underwear friends are treasures who enrich my life. They make a difference in God's work and my life. Without underwear friends, the gospel cannot go into all the world. I am a better servant because of them. Side by side in the battle, we draw strength from each other to serve our Lord together.

I thank God for my underwear friends who lift, support, squeeze, and even pinch me if necessary. They are God's provision to gird me up.

Take Shape

- ❖ **Verse to Ponder:**

    "Thou hast girded me with strength unto the battle" (Psalm 18:39 KJV).

- ❖ **Question:**

Are you an underwear friend? Does God use your friends to gird you with strength?

❖ **Today's Exercise:**

Treadmill exercise is friendly fitness. It gives you the option for interval training. It allows you to walk, jog, and run. Some treadmills have special features such as step counters and heart rate monitors to track fitness progress. Each of our friends has special features. God equips us with gifts and talents to bless each other. One of the benefits of treadmill exercise is that it tightens muscles. As we tread through life together as friends, we gird others' soul muscles—our souls knit and tighten together.

Tread (mill) daily with God and move the mountain of loneliness—He is always treading with us and girds us up. He brings underwear friends into our lives to tread through the good times and bad with us.

God's Relationships
Much More Than Money

If ever there were a pastor to admire, it would be John Davis. He is caring, funny, and wise. He preaches the gospel not only on Sunday mornings or in church services, but through his life. He has a number of health issues that would have knocked any other pastor out of the pulpit, but not John. After three heart attacks, a kidney transplant, diabetes and other ailments, he continued to pastor one of the largest Baptist churches in our home area—with remarkable zeal. The church's newsletter, *The Baptist Beacon*, uses Isaiah 30:17 with a lighthouse as their logo—this man and this church have been a beacon on a hill in Pennsylvania for many years. By his side always is his beautiful and faithful wife, Kathy. Her ministry with children and women completes their call to serve the Lord. Together they shine for God.

God's Sense of Humor

We met Pastor John when we were raising support to return to Bolivia in 1996. A friend told us to call him. We did, and what a blessed meeting it turned out to be. We sat in his office, practically knee to knee because of all the construction materials stacked high while the church was building an addition. The room was no bigger than a closet.

We handed him our brochure and prayer card. I had dark hair on one picture and blonde in the other (I'd recently covered the gray). He immediately quipped, "Which one of these people should our church consider for support?"

"You can support both of them if you like."

Immediately we formed a connection, and for the rest of the meeting, he and I joked while my husband kept trying to interrupt to tell about our ministry.

Finally, Pastor John remarked to Chuck, "I really like *her*, but you are just too serious."

Two days later the phone rang, it was Pastor John wanting to tell us personally that the board had approved us for support. He and the church have remained some of our most faithful supporters. Not only is the support financial, but Pastor John always uplifts and encourages us with his humor and love of the Lord. He and the church give us love, friendship, faithfulness, and an example by which to live.

In Our Hearts

Three years ago, God called Pastor John and Kathy to another ministry. They say they are retiring, but we who know them realize they will never retire from the Lord's work. God will continue to use them wherever He plants them.

Yes, we already miss them in Pennsylvania, but we are thankful for their service and the privilege of knowing them. God bless you, Pastor John and Kathy! We love you! You are in our hearts forever!

Take Shape

❖ **Verse to Ponder:**
"I thank my God upon every remembrance of you" (Philippians 1:3).

❖ **Question:**

The King James translation of Isaiah 30:17 says, "One thousand *shall flee* at the rebuke of one; at the rebuke of five shall ye flee: till ye be left as a beacon upon the top of a mountain, and as an ensign on a hill." Is your light shining as a beacon on a hill as Isaiah 30:17 says? When family, friends, and co-workers think of you, do they always thank God for you? Do you shine light that shapes their souls with brightness?

❖ **Today's Exercise:**

Water Aerobics is a popular bonding activity for family and friends. Younger generations enjoy the fun of swimming pools, and older generations benefit from this sport by maintaining a moderate level of physical fitness. Surely you can agree, Pastor John is popular with all ages, and all generations benefit from his refreshing splash of integrity and humor.

Water Aerobics with God splashes love to the souls around us and moves the mountain of age difference. God plunges us into the bond of fellowship that is not limited by age, group, or skill. It encourages thankfulness.

God's Humor
A Flushed Face

Have you been in a new group where you don't fit in? Imagine being dropped into a new culture and new language. You only know a few phrases in the language of the group and you know little of their culture. Now, imagine my "new" group.

Hand in the Bag

When we were still learning the culture and language, I was invited to a Bible study for women of the local church. It was in a home across the road from the school where we worked. The setting was a rural area of Bolivia, far from civilization. The wind was whipping, and the dust burned my eyes as we approached the house. There I was, the new missionary, sitting in a mud house, with mud floors and with people who spoke a different language, but they loved the same God I did.

No one told me the normal routine of the study. I

didn't understand much of the conversation in Spanish. I sat smiling at everyone and acting as though I knew every word being said.

A small cloth bag was passed to me, and I assumed it was refreshment time. After all, that's what we do in our culture—eat together at those fun ladies' groups. I dipped my hand in and searched for the cookies or candy. I took my time looking for the goodies, but none could be found.

Everyone was howling; they couldn't control their laughter. I assumed I missed the punch line because I didn't understand their Spanish joke. When the ladies finally controlled themselves, I learned the bag was the collection bag, and I, the missionary, looked as though I was taking out of the bag instead of putting into the bag.

My face was flushed. My ego was bruised. But suddenly, I wasn't the missionary; I was a friend with whom they could laugh. The ladies bonded with me because I laughed with them, and friendships were made to further the gospel.

No Embarrassment with Friends

Over the years, these ladies became my most intimate friends—in spite of language and cultural differences. One of them reminded me of the first time she came to my door selling tomatoes from her garden. I chose a few tomatoes and asked her (in my best Spanish) to wait because I wanted to hit her. Yes, a language blunder that could have frightened her and sent her dashing for her life. But she knew the language blunders of new missionaries. Instead of telling her I wanted to pay her, (*pagar* in Spanish), I told her I wanted to *pegar* her—hit her.

These ladies taught me how to live in their country—everything from cooking to the routine of church services to yes, ladies' meetings. I learned to be a friend cross-culturally with their help and love, and many laughs along the way.

Even in our home country, we sometimes feel out of place, unloved, and without friendship that bonds. But being a friend opens the doors of friendship and laughter breaks down the walls of self-consciousness and shyness. When we open up to others, they open up to us. I've learned no matter your geography, "A man who hath friends must show himself friendly" (Proverbs 18:24 KJV).

Take Shape

❖ **Verse to Ponder:**
"A cheerful heart is a good medicine" (Proverbs 17:17).

❖ **Question:**
Do you make your friends smile or laugh just thinking of you? How can you promote bonding with others by laughing together?

❖ **Today's Exercise:**
Laugh. It exercises your lungs and your relationships! Laughter is better than therapy, and it is exercise for good health of body and soul. According to Mayo Clinic, laughing solidifies friendships and makes people feel included. It fosters connection and compassion. It's a great positive coping skill and a universal language. When we laugh together, we create a positive bond. This bond

acts as a buffer against stress, disagreements, and disappointment. Laughing at yourself promotes freedom from self-consciousness. We dig deep into our soul's joy of being ourselves. And, laughing with others is more powerful than laughing alone—because it binds us together.

Laugh with God and move the mountain of self-consciousness.

God's Heart
Not of This World

The phone rang at 8:00 AM. The voice asked in the Quechua language, "How are you? What are you doing?" It was our neighbor and friend, Emilio. Just a week before, Emilio had called to scold me for not letting him know my husband was seriously ill. He is our age—senior discount age—and has been our best friend for twenty-five years. He helped to build the church and introduced us to the community where we now live. He is always checking on us, because as he says, "We are family."

A Diverse Family

Family? Yes. But not the kind of family you might expect. We are the only foreigners working on our side of the city. You can't miss us in a crowd of short, dark-haired people—our hair is white and we are tall.

Emilio also is the president of our community, a

prestigious position. He would have been called Chief a hundred years ago, but in modern society, he is known as President. He is unusually tall for a Bolivian, and his strikingly handsome appearance makes him stand out in a crowd. On most days, you can see Emilio walking his cows to the fields for grazing. He wears sandals, clothes fit for milking (old and ragged), and a large cowboy hat. He is one of the wealthiest among the people in the area because he owns many acres of land and many cows.

A Loving Family

This morning, I told Emilio I was getting ready to go to town to visit my husband in the clinic. He said he wanted to go with me. I would have to pick him up at a meeting two towns away from ours. Problems in that area were mounting, and Emilio is not only a prominent figure in our community, but in the surrounding communities.

We agreed to meet on the road where the meeting was being held. When I saw a gathering of hundreds of people, I knew I had arrived at the site of the meeting. I followed the aroma of the chicken soup cooking in large iron pots, and went to find Emilio. It never occurred to me that I was walking into a political meeting—I was just in a crowd of friends. As foreigners, we are not permitted to take part in any political matters. There I was, the tall blonde *gringa*, in the middle of the meeting. I realized our visas could be revoked just for being in a meeting such as this one.

I hurried back to the car to wait for Emilio. When he got into the car, he said, "Everyone loves to have you around, they all love you and Carlos." That is a love that transcends culture and language. It's a language of love, not of this world, but of a higher realm.

An Eternal Family

Emilio may speak a different language and have a different culture, but for me, his words were God's language of love—straight from God's heart. That day, I knew we were blessed to know and receive heaven's love from God's people whether or not we look alike or speak a different language.

In our own culture and country and world, we find diversity and cultural differences, and even prejudice and bigotry. But God's love transcends our differences and paves the way for the love native to His higher realm to enter our earthly world.

Take Shape

- ❖ **Verse to Ponder:**

    "Dear friends, let us love one another, for love comes from God" (1 John 4:7).

- ❖ **Question:**

    How do you experience heaven's love—love from God? How does God's love shape your soul?

- ❖ **Today's Exercise:**

    Aerobics boosts your high-density lipoprotein (HDL), the "good" cholesterol, and lowers your low-density lipoprotein (LDL), the "bad" cholesterol. This results in less buildup of plaque in your arteries. According to *Mayo Clinic Daily,* a stronger heart doesn't need to beat as fast. A stronger heart also pumps blood more efficiently, which improves blood flow to all parts of the body. Similarly, "working out" with God lowers the "bad" and increases the "good" in us so our spiritual heart works efficiently to eliminate the plaque of sin, becomes stronger, and beats in rhythm with God's heart.

Aerobics with God moves the mountain of plaque from our soul so that His love flows freely to the whole body of Christ—manifesting His heart to the world.

God's Voice

A Voice from the Grave

We have two ponies on our property—Rocky and Adrienne. Their similarities to the personalities of their famous namesakes, Rocky Balboa and his wife, are remarkable. Rocky is strong, and a fighter; Adrienne is weak and prone to illness.

Adrienne was a year old when we adopted her. She lost her beautiful mountain resort home when her owners declared bankruptcy. When she arrived at our house, she was frail, skinny, and scruffy; about the size of our St. Bernard.

Within weeks after her arrival, Adrienne developed Laminitis, a hoof disease that is usually fatal. That is when we met Michael, who became our horseman. In our area of Bolivia there are no horse veterinarians. Michael never completed studies to become a veterinarian, but he had years of experience with sick horses.

We doubted that Adrienne would survive, but

with a few months of Michael's treatment and our prayers, her hoof healed. Michael continued to care for Adrienne and her sidekick, Rocky, for the next few years. Then, a job opportunity presented itself in another city— Michael couldn't resist the salary. We were sad to see him go.

We had developed a long-term friendship with Michael and his family. We talked about the Lord and invited them to our church. Suddenly, we had no contact, until we received a phone call from his daughter a few months after their departure from our city. She was sobbing—someone had died. Who died? Her Poppy. It was a shock to us. Michael was in his late thirties and strong as a horse, excuse the pun. It was a heart attack.

We hung up and immediately wondered about his salvation. Had he ever accepted the Lord? Were we sure he was in heaven? Oh, if we could just have one more minute with him. But it was too late.

More than a year passed with no word from the family until one day, eerie as it seemed, we received a call—from Michael! The voice asked if he could come visit. You can imagine our shock and confusion. We had to tell him, "We thought you were dead".

"Oh, no, it was my father who died last year. My daughter always called us both Poppy." Somewhat of a relief as we still couldn't grasp the reality of his apparent rise from the grave—in our minds, of course.

We anxiously awaited his visit. On his arrival, after the hugs and tears of happiness subsided, we sat in our living room and told him of our grief and our doubts as to where he was in eternity. Right there on that day, he accepted the Lord. It wasn't too late, and we were thankful for one more chance to talk with him. It wasn't a voice from the grave, but a voice that called out to Jesus for salvation. We knew for sure where he would spend eternity.

We don't know what tomorrow will bring. Michael's story jolted me into *the now*. Tomorrow may be too late for words, and I may never get another chance to talk to a voice from the grave.

Take Shape

- ❖ **Verse to Ponder:**

    "At just the right time, I heard you. On the day of salvation, I helped you. Indeed, the "right time" is *now*. Today is the day of salvation" (2 Corinthians 6:2 NLT).

- ❖ **Question:**

    Will you begin to exercise your soul's faith *now*? Tomorrow may be too late to start. Listen to God's voice calling you *now*.

- ❖ **Today's Exercise:**

    Boxing is said to be your best friend for losing weight. Its benefits include fat burning, increased muscle tone, building strong bones, and improved core stability, according to *Dynamic Boxing Fitness*. In short, you lose a lot of unwanted baggage by boxing.

    Conversely, the Bible says Jesus is your best friend; but with Him you never lose. Jesus is your best friend who keeps (saves) you from losing a home in heaven for eternity. You only gain with Him—not unwanted weight, but a glorious eternity.

Boxing with God and His Son, your best friend, moves the mountain of separation from God and assures that your soul will be in shape to arrive at your final destination—your eternal home in heaven. Listen to His voice now and gain eternal life so beyond the grave you'll hear His sweet voice forever.

God's Nature
Finding Falling Waters

The hill seemed like a mountain to me. I gasped with each breath and wondered if it were my last. As you'll recall, I'm not an athletic person, nor do I enjoy engaging in outings that drain my energy. I need a lot of persuasion and a worthwhile reason to set out on a challenging adventure. And this wasn't just any hike. This one led me into the wilds of the Andes Mountains.

A Hike to Remember

On that day a few years back, I couldn't say no (but almost did) to the young people's request to show me the beauty of their home turf. Our youth group took my husband and me on a hike to see a stunning site that not many on this earth are blessed to behold. We were skeptical. It started from our rural church; and things got tough from there. Our trek would take us into the wilds, up a mountain, and deep

into a wooded area. I remember thinking not even
Indiana Jones would seek this place out to visit.
Would the destination be worth the journey?

You're a missionary, I kept repeating to myself.
*Buck up! Yes Lord, I knew there'd be days like this.
You can help me show these kiddos I'm willing to put
them above my fears and weakness. Maybe, just
maybe, they'll see Your strength in me.*

I don't know about strength, but I'm sure they
saw my physical weakness. I slipped and fell into a
cactus. Squatting to rise and continue, I felt the
jabbing of prickly needles pinch my arms. Drops of
blood streamed down. Okay, that's an exaggeration.
They were only specks of blood, but the wound felt as
if someone drove a stake in my arm. I brushed my
hand across my face, and red sweat appeared on my
hand. Was that blood too? Would this be the story of
my martyrdom on the mission field?

The group burst into laughter. Why? Because it
was the white powder from the cactus plant that
changed into a natural red dye when mixed with
water, or sweat in my case. It was the same red dye

produced by the tiny bugs that caused havoc for a coffee company not too long ago. I had to laugh, as well.

I kept wondering how much farther I'd have to trek into the wilds, until the moment we saw this eighth wonder of the world.

Suddenly, the roar of cascading water in a distance signaled we were close. The fresh fragrance of nature relaxed my nerves. And then the towering palms parted. A spectacular waterfall jutted out from the rocky landscape. I forgot the throbbing arm and burning muscles, as I basked in this awe-inspiring wonder of God's creation.

Be Open to the Hikes of Life

What did I learn from this experience? Take all opportunities presented to you to explore and enjoy the wonders of our world. Conquer your fears and your frailty; trust in God's strength—not your own—and step out to experience life. Step out of your comfort zone, trust God, and watch Him do wonders in your life.

My hike proved well worth the agony of aching muscles to behold God's pristine nature. It cemented a bond with those teens that will last a lifetime. Many opened their hearts to God after that trip.

If we remain paralyzed by the fear of what might go wrong (exhaustion, sore muscles), we'll never experience all that will go right (in this case: new souls in eternity). Yes, it's worth it now and worth it throughout eternity!

Take Shape

- **Verse to Ponder:**

   "I'll refresh tired bodies; I'll restore tired souls" (Jeremiah 31:25 MSG).

- **Question:**

   Will your difficult journey through this life be worth the sacrifices in the end? Where is your destination? Do you trust in God's refreshment and restoration?

- **Today's Exercise:**

   Squats. The muscle stretching we get from doing squats gets the blood pumping through our bodies. Good circulation means more nutrients and oxygen reach our vital organs and muscles and our tired bodies are refreshed. Just as squats increase circulation of our physical bodies, spiritual squats lift us out of complacency and pump our souls with God's oxygen, His Spirit, so we engage with others and increase the circulation of His message. By stretching outside our comfort zones, we circulate through the body of Christ and give spiritual nutrition and new breath to shape souls. God refreshes us and restores our souls—and the souls of those near us. When we hit our limits or fall down, let's squat to rise up and go beyond our comfort zone to circulate God's nutrients through our spiritual gifts.

Squats with God will move the mountain of spiritual isolation so that our souls reach outside our borders of comfort and circulate new breath to the body of Christ.

God's Workers
Are You the Missionary's Wife?

I like to dress up, eat out, and shop—some of my delights on furlough. I'm still a girl—in my mind and my heart. Does that surprise you? Try to let go of the myths you've developed over the years and allow me to reveal the real life of a missionary woman.

Remember a missionary shares many of your same struggles. You may find her to be lonely, not fitting into a fast-changing culture, and drained from the pressures put on her to be super spiritual. Maybe God will challenge you to be a friend to her while she is on the home front.

What Every Woman Needs

Often, women avoid her because they don't want to expose themselves to her. They may fear she will be critical of their way of life, or envious of their beautiful homes and blessed lives in their homeland. Nothing could be farther from the truth. And, if you are a missionary woman reading this book, I hope you'll find freedom with my words.

Occasionally, I get asked the question, "Are you the missionary's wife"? My answer, "Yes, and he's the missionary's husband." I've seen many missionaries leave the field because the wife is unhappy. She feels she is of no value. Other missionary women may not be aware of her suffering because she is too embarrassed to tell anyone how miserable she is. Women are vital to the team. It takes both husband and wife if a married couple is to minister on a foreign field. Likewise, single missionaries are crucial to building of the Kingdom. They bring special gifts and talents that bless all who minister with them. We all have a part in the overall picture—those working on the field and those who send us—men and women.

During our missionary training, we studied the Bible, learned to live among tribal people, and prepared to translate unwritten languages and plant churches. We even had a medical course to prepare us for living in uncivilized areas. I never realized how valuable that training would be until we faced health issues while living in places where there were no medical facilities.

Wherever You Are, Make It Home

As part of our training, we built and lived in a plastic house for six weeks—deep in the woods of Pennsylvania with no access to the outside world. We had to survive with the supplies we took with us. I baked bread in a mud oven, took showers from a bucket of water pouring over my head and hung my prettiest white curtains on windows of screen. It was home. I learned an important lesson for my future missionary life—wherever you are, make it home.

Long before we touched down in Bolivia, our first days of living as missionaries-in-training in a dorm situation initiated moments of intense conflict between my heart and God's heart. Having sold our dream house, we left a lucrative business to work at Sandy Cove Ministries, a Bible conference center in North East, Maryland. After one year on staff there, we sold everything and entered missionary training.

Adjustment and *Change* became our new names.

One afternoon, soon after our arrival at the mission institute, I sat in the library filing prayer requests from missionaries on the field—my job when I had free time from classes. The ladies helping me were chatting about future plans regarding their prospective fields of service. As we exchanged tips and recipes, I said the unthinkable. "When I was home, I used to can a lot." The looks of shock and one rather blunt comment caused my eye to twitch.

"You are home," slipped from one woman's not-so-smiley face. I hadn't accepted our two-room apartment, communal bathrooms, and laundry rooms filled with wringer washers as my home. To me, this was just a place to be educated as a missionary to further the Kingdom in a foreign land.

I wrestled with God daily, just wanting to get this part of the journey over and move on. God heard my prayers. "Because he bends down to listen, I will pray as long as I have breath!" (Psalm 116:2 NLT). As the months went on, I came to realize this would be the rest of my life—moving from one place to another. It was then I internalized Jim Elliot's quote, "Wherever you are, be all there." And so the transition began. I began desiring to bend with God as He shaped my soul for His purpose and plan.

Take It to the Ends of the Earth

If we don't make our nest home, the twigs and hay in it will aggravate us. We will never be content anywhere we live—missionary or not. I have packed and unpacked hundreds of times; but since that day in the dorm, I've unpacked and made it home. I've taken curtains, plaques, and knickknacks with me everywhere—even to the jungle. If you move down the street, or across town, or to another state or country, never leave your personal things behind if you can help it. They are part of you.

The missionary women I've seen suffer the most are those who never made the field home, for one reason or another. I hang my curtains, put up my decorations, and light candles—home. I'm blessed with friends who see me as a person, a woman, and a soul who needs to be shaped. They even buy me things to decorate my house and clothes to make me *not* look like a missionary, and all kinds of other sweet and practical items—one reason our luggage bulges when returning to the field from our furloughs. Some even give us gifts to pay for our baggage. They shape my soul with love because they care that I look stylish and that I am at home wherever I am. God's love on earth flows through His people; I'm a recipient of that love.

In our worship services during training, we often sang a hymn that still rings in my heart. "*I will go to the ends of the earth*." Sometimes, I stop to think about where I am. I look out my window at the magnificent, rugged vista. Yep, I'm at the ends of the earth. But I am home.

Take Shape

❖ **Verse to Ponder:**
"I rejoiced in the Lord greatly that once again you renewed your care for me. You were, in fact, concerned about me but lacked the opportunity to show it. I don't say this out of

need, for I have learned to be content in whatever circumstances I am. I know both how to have a little, and I know how to have a lot. In any and all circumstances I have learned the secret of being content—whether well fed or hungry, whether in abundance or in need. I am able to do all things through Him who strengthens me. Still, you did well by sharing with me in my hardship" (Philippians 4:10–13).

❖ **Question:**

Are you living a life of contentment? How?

❖ **Today's Exercise**:

Bending. Exercise should first improve our ability to manage daily life. Functional flexibility is a fitness level that allows us to climb stairs, tie our shoes, pick up a bag of groceries, reach the top shelf, get in and out of a car, and sprint for the bus. Bending exercises stretch and strengthen muscles used in activities of daily life (ADL). A University of Wisconsin La Crosse Exercise and Health

Program study tested exercises that imitated the bending and reaching moves typical of ADL and found agility, dynamic balance and shoulder flexibility increased significantly in test subjects. Similarly, bending our soul—being flexible as God moves us through life's changing circumstances—can improve our daily life for activities of godly living (AGL) and help us find contentment in every circumstance.

Bending with God can move the mountain of discontentment, so our souls will be flexible and content, and our AGL will improve exponentially.

God's Dogs
A Slobbery Dog's Purpose

After one of our furloughs, we returned to Bolivia and our children's ministry. Our welcome home gift from a friend awaited us—a Saint Bernard puppy. A slobbery, chubby fur ball. We weren't looking for a puppy and certainly not one that would turn into doggy King Kong. Yet, we couldn't refuse such a warm gesture from a cherished friend, and the puppy *was* irresistible.

The day after his arrival, tragedy struck in the U.S.A.—9-11. Glued to the TV with the puppy cuddled on my lap, I watched the horrific scene. That's how George, named in honor of President George Bush, became a lap dog.

George eventually weighed in at 180 pounds and stood four feet tall, a massive dog with the personality of Beethoven (the dog from the old movie). Yet he remained a lap dog. He became our children's ministry mascot. Kids enrolled in our computer classes just to play with George.

Fulfilling God's Purpose

Over the years, we've come to understand God has a purpose for every event—large and small. On the large side, God had a purpose for Christ's life and death—our free gift of salvation. On the small side, God had a purpose for a 180-pound, slobbering fur ball. George slobbered love on all and brought joy to hundreds of kids who entered our classes. It didn't matter if the faces his tongue washed were dirty, or if the children's clothes were ragged. He loved them all, regardless of skin color, language barriers, or cultural differences. He became a role model for me, a glimpse of Christ's unconditional love.

The kids who attended our programs during George's lifetime have grown up, but they carry the memories of George's selfless love. They also remember Bible lessons learned while they were covered in doggy slobber.

When George had nearly finished God's eternal purpose for him, tragedy struck again. This time, it was George's tragedy—a brain tumor. Soon, the children's giggles ceased, and smiles turned into tears. But the children who received the gift of salvation have happy souls today and forever.

Like George, we have an eternal purpose on earth. Will I fulfill God's purpose for my life and exemplify God's unconditional love as George did? Will I be remembered with such love when I'm gone? Will you?

Take Shape

- ❖ **Verse to Ponder:**

    "According to his eternal purpose which he accomplished in Christ Jesus our Lord" (Ephesians 3:11 NIV).

- ❖ **Question:**

    How do you find purpose each day, each month, each year? What's your purpose today?

- ❖ **Today's Exercise:**

    Walk the Dog. Sometimes, while you're walking the dog, it walks you. I experienced that often while walking George, who outweighed me. Suddenly, I'd be headed in a different direction flying behind the dog—feet in the air. Life is like that. We set out to accomplish a purpose and don't fulfill it.

Walking the Dog can help us stay on track to complete our purpose. I determine to accomplish my eternal purpose by keeping my eyes fixed on the goal of following Jesus Christ who accomplished His goal and gives us the power to accomplish our purpose for Him.

God's Bread
Mud Oven Ministry

When Thanksgiving becomes a memory, we always look forward to Christmas. In the United States, storekeepers decorate throughout December, while in homes, shopping lists get longer and longer. Neighborhoods glisten with decorated trees that twinkle in windows, and kitchens everywhere overflow with scents of freshly baked cookies.

But the scene is different where I live.

My first thoughts of Christmas are not of sugarplums or decorations, not even of cookies or candy. My first thought is bread. Not just any bread, but bread baked in a mud oven. If you've never had a fresh, warm bun out of a mud oven, you are missing a delicacy. The aroma rising from the oven, the crackling fire, and of course, the first bite when your teeth smile as that bread glides over your taste buds. Bread is a Christmas blessing to many where I live in Bolivia.

Ministering to Children at Christmas

The world seems to put more emphasis on gifts, food, and decorations at Christmas than on the birth of our Savior. But Christians focus on the birth of Christ, and why He was born. Many take part in children's ministries in the U.S. and around the world at this time. They give of their resources so those less fortunate will be blessed with gifts at Christmas. As for me, Christmas *does* mean the giving of gifts and food, and yes, even bread. I am blessed to have a part of a ministry for children who otherwise may never receive gifts.

But my greater joy is that with the gift giving comes an opening to share the Christmas Story, and the greatest Gift of all, with the people and children of the Andes Mountains of Bolivia. Most of them have never heard about Jesus or how He was born in a stable and died on a cross for them.

Every Christmas, we travel with our Bolivian church members to remote mountain regions. We take gifts and food to families living without even the most basic needs. There are no twinkling lights or

Christmas trees in their small, mud homes because there is no electricity; most don't even have firewood.

So, we buy toys for the children. Little trucks and baby dolls make their eyes pop with joy. We wash feet, cut nails, wash hair, and remove lice from little heads. The little girls' eyes widen, and their lips curl upward when we tie bows and ribbons in their clean hair. Then the fun part comes. We reach into big burlap bags filled with *mountains* of bread and pull out the most wanted gift that everyone has come to receive. Bread. Shouts of joy and lines of fidgeting feet wait for their treasured delicacy.

The Bread of Life

Can you imagine asking a child you know whether he wants more bread or just candy, and he answers, "Just bread, please"? Yet that is what we hear.

Each Christmas, we set out to give gifts to needy children. Their eyes light up when they see the gifts and candy, but what they want most is the bread. Imagine what a treat this is in the high mountains above the tree line where there is no firewood to use in baking.

Then the small children hear the story of Jesus for the first time. They accept the gift of salvation joyfully and without hesitation. What a joy and privilege this is. A highlight of our year.

Yes, we give Christmas gifts to children who have nothing and are elated to receive a morsel of bread. But, better yet, is the joy of seeing them receive the Bread of Life for their souls and become children of God.

For me, Christmas will forever mean giving away bread baked in a mud oven alongside the living Bread from heaven. As we feed their tummies with mud-oven bread and their souls with the Bread of Life, and God shapes their souls for eternity.

Take Shape

- ❖ **Verse to Ponder**:

    "I am the bread of life. He who comes to me will never go hungry" (John 6:35 NLT).

❖ **Question**:

How do you feed your soul and the souls of others?

❖ **Today's Exercise:**

Ice skating Christmas scenes warm our hearts. While I recall the joy of seeing smiling faces of underprivileged children receiving gifts and eating mud-oven bread, you probably think of ice skating in Central Park, families sitting by the fire, and Christmas church and school programs. Ice skating is fun. It is also an aerobic exercise great for cardiovascular health. The best part about skating is you get a cardio workout without even realizing it. The best part about giving of ourselves selflessly is that our hearts and those hearts receiving the gifts don't even realize the workout taking place in our souls—changing hard hearts to soft and seeing pliable hearts massaged by God's hands.

Ice skating with God changes our heart

condition and moves the mountain of poverty and suffering.

God's Hand
Walk on Water

I will always be grateful for the memories, spiritual growth, and friendships formed in our first year in full-time ministry at Sandy Cove Ministries—a privilege and a blessing. In this picturesque setting we served God alongside dedicated staff members, and we had the privilege of sitting in on sessions taught by both famous and notable Spirit-led Bible scholars. If you've never had the joy of visiting this Spirit-filled, tranquil nook on the Chesapeake Bay, you are missing one of God's blessings this side of heaven. Should you have the opportunity to visit, you'll notice a sign when you enter the conference grounds. You can't miss it—it's huge. It says, "Jesus Never Fails." By the time you leave, those words will be etched on your heart.

Walk on the Water

Chuck and I walked hand-in-hand to the bayside

dock many nights. Not long after we moved there, our first visitors arrived from our home area in Pennsylvania. They loved the bayside view at sunset. They'd been good friends for many years, and of course, we laughed together often. When their visit was coming to an end, I suggested we all go for one last walk to the pier, but that wasn't what I said. Instead, I blurted, "Let's go walk on the water."

My loving friend responded, "Oh, now that you're in full-time Christian ministry you can walk on water?" That evoked a good laugh! But the disciples didn't laugh when they saw Jesus walking on the water. In fact, they were terrified and thought Jesus was a ghost. "When the disciples saw Him walking on water, they were terrified" (Matthew 14:26 NLT).

I have to confess. I know the Bible says God works all things for good, but sometimes I too am terrified about my circumstances just like the disciples were—when I am not walking by faith.

"Then Peter went over the side of the boat and walked on water toward Jesus" (Matthew 14:29b NIV). There he was, walking on water going toward

Jesus. He experienced God's power. Can you imagine the scene? Wind blowing, waves splashing, but Peter wasn't thinking about his surroundings. He was just caught up with looking at Jesus. But then he saw the wind, the Bible says. Yes, he looked at the wind and not at Jesus. He took his eyes off the Lord and instead, looked at his circumstances, and he began to sink. His faith faltered. He cried out for the Lord to save him.

And then the Scripture says, "Jesus immediately reached out his hand and grabbed him" (Matthew14:31 NLT). Jesus didn't let Peter sink. He reached out and caught him—immediately. And what about Peter? When he focused on the high winds and waves, his faith faltered. But what he did next is significant. He looked to Jesus for help. While the waves pulled Peter down, his hand reached out to Jesus, and Jesus caught him. Peter was afraid, but he looked to Jesus for help. He had faith that Jesus would help him.

Eyes Fixed on Jesus

At times, we splash through the winds and waves of difficult circumstances. To maintain our faith when we are thrashed about, we must keep our eyes on Jesus and not our circumstances. Sometimes our faith may falter, and we may begin to sink, but Jesus will always be there to stretch out His hand and pull us out of the waves. Sometimes the winds howl around us, and other times they die down. But whether in the boat or on the water tossed about in the waves, we know we are safe because "Jesus never fails!" And, with our eyes fixed on Jesus, we *can* walk on water.

Take Shape

- ❖ **Verse to Ponder**:
    "And when they climbed into the boat, the wind stopped" (Matthew 14:32 NLT).
- ❖ **Question:**
    Are you walking on water today or sinking? On what (or whom) are the eyes of your heart fixed?

❖ **Today's Exercise:**

Scuba Diving. Scuba diving helps keep your lungs fit. During a dive, you have to take in as much air as possible. As you strive to breathe air from your oxygen tank, you also exercise your lungs by expanding them to absorb more oxygen, according to *The Random Science*. If divers surrender to the flow of the current instead of fighting it, they sense a feeling of calmness and of being at home in the water. When we are terrified like the disciples were, we need to force fear out of our hearts and instead surrender and feel the calmness. Just as oxygen fills our lungs and keeps them fit, so our soul is filled with calmness when we allow God's oxygen (His Spirit) to flow through us. Our soul's lungs expand. Next time you sink to deep waters, breathe the oxygen of the Holy Spirit and see how your soul will stay calm and fit. You will be at home with Jesus.

Scuba Diving with God fills our soul's lungs with the oxygen of the Holy Spirit and moves the mountain of fear.

God's Senior Citizens
Senior Teenagers

Teens sometimes want to run away from home when their parents restrict their activities. They balk at delicious and nutritious food set before them. They rebel when their driving privileges suddenly and abruptly end for a few weeks. And, how about an early bedtime? No child wants that to happen. And when they rebel, they get grounded. Ouch!

Just as teenagers experience grounding, so do senior citizens—I found this out personally when Chuck and I were both scheduled for surgeries. We were blessed to be senior teenagers for a few weeks—enjoying all the blessings of a timeout. But at first, we liked it just about as much as a teen appreciates his first grounding.

We Got Grounded!

It began without warning, and quickly escalated into a state of frenzy. While talking to a friend after the initial shock of it all, I told her I felt like a teenager under restrictions who wanted to jump in the parents' car and run away—heading to Walmart no doubt. Nevertheless, we both ended up enjoying our season of grounding—not easy for two people who can't sit still. We never expected a stop moment in our lives—a time of letting go. I expected to take care of Chuck for a few days after his surgery, and then I'd relax in his care for me after my first cataract surgery. I was planning on milking it for as long as I could.

Chuck's surgery evolved into a major operation that his surgeon likened to heart bypass. We had no idea of the risk until five minutes before the procedure when it escalated from an outpatient procedure to a major surgery. The only comfort was that this never surprised God.

Had I known the risks before that morning, I would have tried to talk Chuck out of it. But how could I keep him from taking the risk to be out of the horrific pain from the nerve damage in his back he'd endured for three years? I couldn't ask him to forego an opportunity to be out of that pain—no matter what fears I had of him potentially being paralyzed from the surgery.

Just days earlier, I'd read this verse; I clung to it through the surgery. "Call to me and I will answer you. I'll tell you marvelous and wondrous things that you could never figure out on your own" (Jeremiah 33:3 NIV). God knew I could never have figured it out on my own. Chuck had peace that passed understanding and told me over and over it would be okay. His faith glowed in the pre-op area.

In the end, the surgeon burned forty-two lesions on Chuck's central nerve. The nerve was damaged, inflamed, and red—all a result of the shingles.

God's plans were different from ours and much better for us, even though our natural man would buck these circumstances. In the weeks that followed, we couldn't leave the house without a driver. I couldn't drive because of my cataracts and Chuck couldn't drive after surgery. Our long-time dear friends insisted we stay with them and made us feel at home in their lovely home.

So, there we were—grounded. Jane, our hostess,

cooked, cleaned, washed our clothes, and drove us where we needed to go. Jim did whatever we needed around the house and drove us to and from Pittsburgh for Chuck's checkups. During the surgery, he sat with me and answered calls because I cried when I tried to explain what was happening.

Let Go!

Some would say God forced us to be still. But I say God tenderly put us in a position to relinquish all to Him. The original Hebrew root of *be still* doesn't mean *be quiet;* it means *let go.* We let go and saw God work. We rested in Him.

It wasn't long before Chuck began walking without the help of a walker or crutches. He used a cane for security when he was outside. His right leg was weak (an aftereffect of the surgery), but the therapist assured us it would strengthen in the weeks ahead when therapy stopped. Sure enough, it did.

Many friends did other wonderful things to help. Blessed abundantly, we are! Some came with food and took turns getting us to appointments. We were all cozy under God's wings. He met our needs and showed us His hand at every turn. He went ahead of us and cleared the way for us to pass through every obstacle—while His wings held us securely.

Chuck and I entered a new season in our lives—one of relinquishing control and resting physically and spiritually. Yes, we felt like senior teenagers, but with thankful hearts that we were driven not driving, fed not cooking, and enjoying early bedtimes that weren't mandatory. All of this in a comfy home with lovely, caring saints, meeting our every need and our wants too—like finding chocolate pie in the fridge.

God answers our prayers. He takes good care of us. He goes ahead and prepares the way. We now realize this grounding was God-ordained; and we're thankful for it.

Be assured. God goes ahead of all His children. Our task may simply be to rest under His everlasting wings.

Take Shape

- ❖ **Verse to Ponder:**

    "The Lord your God is a devouring fire;" (Deuteronomy 4:24 NLT).

- ❖ **Question:**

    How do you (or don't you) relinquish control to God?

- ❖ **Today's Exercise:**

    Diddly-squats. Have you ever done diddly-squat? It's not easy. You must relinquish your will to God's will. Stop. Listen. Rest. Focus on God. Let go. Think of the last time you wanted someone's attention and they seemed distracted and only politely pretended to be interested in what you had to say. Now, imagine how God feels when we don't give Him attention. He takes good care of us and goes ahead of us in life like a devouring fire. Doing diddly-squat may be the *most* we can do for God—putting everything aside to spend time with Him—letting go of our control. The muscle stretching that we get from doing physical squats gets blood pumping throughout our body. Doing diddly-squat allows the Holy Spirit to circulate through our soul, pumping the nutrients of His Word to build us up for life's battles. We rest in His presence to fuel our souls for service.

Diddly-squat with God stops the noise of earth so we can hear the Voice of Heaven and move the mountain of self-control and self-centeredness. We become God controlled and soul centered—shaped for service.

God's Food
Bedtime with Basil

You may think this is a story about Basil the cat (or dog), it's not. It's not even an animal story, although I enjoy writing those stories for children. I do have cats and dogs and even a special-needs cat, Quasimodo. He will be a good story for another day. And, by the way, he looks like the real Quasimodo. He has a humped back, walks with a limp, and is famous in our neighborhood. But this is about basil, the stuff you put in spaghetti sauce and on pizza. And no, there's not even a recipe involved.

So, let's talk about mosquitos, that's right, the bugs. We have plenty of bugs in Bolivia and on occasion have slept with them. A few years ago, we bought a new mattress and got more for our money than expected—bugs included. After days of clawing our skin and drawing blood—making the itch even worse—we thought to turn the mattress. What an incredibly intelligent idea! There they were looking up at us from their comfy bed—hundreds of them. They weren't bedbugs, but tiny bugs that would have eventually devoured us—a bedtime horror story. That problem was easily solved but not so with our problem of a mosquito infestation during our rainy season.

This bedtime story is about mosquitoes. Our rainy season began with a downpour that year, and mosquitos became our renters paying their bill with nights of buzzing misery in our bed and around our heads. When we ventured outside in the night air, we opened and closed the door quickly, first making sure the lights were out. That isn't easy for senior citizens who always try to avoid a dangerous fall. We'd bundle up as if we were in Alaska even though our temperatures reached the 90's. But we never ventured outside before stuffing our pockets with dryer sheets —we'd heard they keep the pests at a distance. Then, and only then, we'd steal out into the night to do whatever it is we had to do—most times to tuck in our ponies.

Thank the Lord we have inside bathrooms; there

were times we didn't in our early years of missionary work. We enjoy indoor plumbing in our golden years—thank You God! By the way, the only golden things we have so far in these senior years are two Golden Retrievers who are so active they are making our golden years not golden, but exhausting. They are not ideal pets for the over-fifty crowd; I'm not even sure our grandkids could keep up with their pace. But their love and affection make up for their hyperactive lifestyle.

Beat the Buzzing

Back to those annoying mosquitoes. Hold on, I am about to give you a lesson on how to beat the bugs, but not literally. We tried that—beating them—and I almost had another broken nose. There were hands flying through the air and newspapers batting in every direction. The mosquitoes must have thought we were dancing in our pajamas. I'd bet they were amused; you would have been.

After trying everything we knew, we retired to bed under the covers, trying not to suffocate, but the buzzing continued. When out of the pitch-black night, I remembered a remedy—anything was worth a try. Basil! I remembered reading an article that said the fragrance of basil is so powerful mosquitoes won't come near it.

Off we went to the kitchen, where we found the large container of basil. Now what? We opened the top and put it directly between our heads, quietly waiting in the dark for the next attack. Nothing! No buzzing! We finally drifted off to dreamland escaping the nightmare. Every night of rainy season, ever since our "dancing with mosquitoes" episode, we have slept peacefully with basil tucked between the headboard and mattress.

Basil for the Enemy

Now wouldn't it be great if we had something like basil to ward off the devil when he buzzes around and won't let us alone? Oh, wait, we do. Basil keeps mosquitoes at a distance, and the Word of God keeps the devil at a distance.

Just like we opened the container of basil and

saw it work, we can open the Word of God and see it work. God gives us all the tools we need to serve Him, we only need to use what is right before us, His Word. Remember how Jesus rebuffed Satan's direct attacks? Three times He told the enemy, "It is written." And then He quoted His Father's Word. (See Luke 4 for the whole scene.)

Let's follow Christ's victorious example. Yes, we can get out the basil to hold off mosquitoes, but of greater significance we can open the Bible to put on our armor to stand against the devil so our souls won't be bitten by the buzzing devil.

Take Shape

❖ **Verse to Ponder:**
"Put on all of God's armor so that you will be able to stand firm against all the strategies of the devil" (Ephesians 6:11 NLT).

❖ **Question:**
When you are surrounded by problems—your mosquitos—do you reach for your Bible—your basil—to stop the enemy from buzzing

around you?

- ❖ **Today's Exercise:**

Cooking burns 150 calories an hour. I count that as an hour of exercise—another exercise I practice daily. I cook 95 percent of our meals at home. Granted, our selection of restaurants is slim due to our location and the safety factor. Now, if a miracle happens and Bolivia imports the fine restaurant of McDonald's or Cracker Barrel, that percentage will decrease dramatically—at least for the first month. I'm sure after that month, we'd need to exercise, diet, and return to cooking at home.

I'm emphasizing that point because fast food restaurants are known to be high in calories and low in nutritional content. Also, the extreme portion size of restaurant meals contributes to weight gain in America.

Preparing meals at home gives us the ability to exercise portion control and curb temptation to overeat. By adding spices for flavor—yes, basil too—and using less sugar and fats, meals at home can be more flavorful and nutritious with fewer calories.

The University of Michigan found eating family meals at the dinner table is associated with fewer psychological issues and higher academic success in children. Cooking at home shapes the souls of children by promoting sociability in the family while spending time together. Spices like basil do more than keep mosquitos from buzzing around your head. They also ward off the pounds from piling around our hips.

Cooking with God moves the mountain of unwanted pounds from an unhealthy lifestyle and keeps our souls in shape. Putting on all God's armor helps us fight the battles of temptation—whatever they may be. We'll lose the flab from our bodies and shape our souls.

God's Strawberries
A Strawberry Shortcake Prayer

I can still envision the pretty tablecloth, fine china, and luscious red strawberries as we sat around the table with dear friends and Jesus. Yes, He sat there among us, in the invisible chair. We could all see Him.

The year was 1977. We were beginning our first year at Sandy Cove. It was there we met and worked with Horace and Carol Sue Perkins, and Bill and Dorothy Montgomery. They ministered in music and many other details for the ministry; such dedicated, talented, precious saints who taught us much about our wonderful Savior. They also were instrumental in our transition into mission work.

God So Near

I remember that day well. Clouds of humidity engulfed the Chesapeake Bay the evening Horace, Carol Sue, Bill, and Dorothy arrived at our home for dinner. Dorothy wrote the Countdown song, still sung by children everywhere; we all sang that song around the table that evening, such precious memories. Between them, they had decades of service to our Lord; we were in the presence of greatness, in a heavenly sense.

As we bowed to give thanks, Horace led in prayer. His sweet, soft voice calmed the air around us as he spoke to the Lord. "Oh, Lord, thank you for these wonderful strawberries, they are so big, and we can't wait to eat them." Everyone chuckled and dug in.

Horace taught us something that evening; it wasn't what he said but rather how he said it. He talked to God as if He were sitting right there with us, in that invisible chair. It was a loving relationship between them, like best friends who talked frequently, laughed together, and knew each other well. God desires that kind of fellowship with us daily; He wants us to include Him in every aspect of our lives, even our strawberry shortcake.

One Life Lived for Jesus

Horace is with the Lord now, maybe enjoying heavenly strawberries. He made a difference in many lives; by his example, he gave me a reborn desire to know more of God every day and to make a difference in lives I touch through everyday living.

As we strive to know Him better daily, through studying His Word and prayer, Jesus will shine through us, so others will come to know Him as Lord and Savior, and as a friend with whom they, too, can eat strawberry shortcake.

Take Shape

- ❖ **Verse to Ponder:**
    "That we may know him and the power of his resurrection" (Philippians 3:10 KJV).
- ❖ **Question:**
    How often do you share strawberry shortcake with the Person in your invisible chair?
- ❖ **Today's Exercise:**
    Smile: According to the Vanderbilt University Medical Center, laughing and smiling lead to

increased heart rate and calorie burning. Finally, an exercise I can smile about! As the heart rate increases, the metabolism increases, so laughing and smiling increase energy consumption. When we smile at a stranger, we appear friendly. New friends can be gained just by our smile. Even in bad situations, I've seen others mimic a smile. When you read about Horace's prayer, I imagine your lips turned upward—right? Being with Jesus makes us smile and makes us attractive—your beauty secret for today. You're welcome! As we spend time with Jesus, others become attracted to our resemblance of Him. His beauty shines through us. The world around us recognizes His presence, even though they may not know Him personally.

Smile with God and move the mountain of unattractiveness. A smile lets the inner beauty of Jesus shine through us. We appear beautiful, while making the world around us more beautiful!

God's Angels
Rental Car Revelation

Whether you fly frequently or not, you may have rented a car on occasion. Booking a rental car online can avoid hassles at your destination. Chuck and I usually rent a vehicle and drive from our hometown in Pennsylvania to Miami when returning to Bolivia. Then, in Miami, we catch a flight to South America. Sounds easy enough. But a few years ago, we not only experienced a *frustrating* encounter when we approached the pickup counter, but we also experienced a *supernatural* encounter in the parking lot of the Pittsburgh Airport.

We searched the internet for the best deal for a vehicle that could accommodate our luggage—a lot of luggage. I should note some of the important stuff we take—pepperoni and Velveeta Cheese. (Necessities we can't get in Bolivia.) Prices were out of sight—$800. Our previous rental cost had been under $200. How could prices have jumped so high?

We could fly for less, but the extra baggage would be expensive, and the airline wouldn't allow that much extra weight. We continued the frantic search in the weeks before our departure date. More prayers!

Our departure date crept closer. Then, one morning a new posting appeared—SUV—one way to Miami $200. The price was right and just the right size for all the stuff we couldn't leave behind.

Prayers answered, we booked it. We packed and planned for the trip to the airport the day before our departure. One of our "underwear friends" offered to drive us to Pittsburgh to pick up the rental.

When we arrived to pick up the vehicle, the clerk informed us we had to go to the main counter at the Pittsburgh Airport because this location did not recognize the offer we'd found online. This should have alarmed us but we didn't question the clerk's explanation. So, we barreled through city traffic to the airport.

Inside the airport, we headed to the rental counter to pick up our unbelievable deal—that should have also been a clue—you know, too good to be true. My husband explained to the attractive lady behind the counter what we'd found online and awaited delivery of the SUV. She checked her computer. There appeared to be no such *deal*. How could that be? We had proof of our credit card receipt of the booking. She'd check again. Nope! Nothing! There had never been such an offer. The only thing available was an SUV for $800, one way, for one day.

Our friend who drove us asked, "What are you going to do?" What could I say? Then these words poured out of my mouth, surprising even me.

"Well, we're not paying $800, and we're not leaving here without a car because tomorrow morning we leave for Florida and the next day to Bolivia. God will have to do a miracle. Everything is already in motion. We need to pray!" Our friend agreed although skeptical. My husband believed as I did, God could do a miracle. So, we prayed, trusting God to intervene. We couldn't see a possible solution, but God saw it all.

God Solves the Problem

Chuck returned to the counter to ask another question. "May I see the SUVs available?"

Her answer was firm. "Yes, you can walk to the parking lot and look at two cars that are available, but the price will be the same, $800."

I'm not sure why my husband agreed to look at two SUVs that we weren't going to rent, other than he followed the lead of the Holy Spirit. He walked to the parking lot. My friend and I stayed seated and prayed. When Chuck returned, he gave me a thumbs-up with a twinkle in his eyes from across the room and then walked to the counter to tell the lady what had occurred in the parking lot.

The lady behind the counter listened intently. He told her that as he strolled through the parking lot an attendant dressed in airport uniform approached him.

"May I help you?" she asked.

My husband told her the story of our dilemma, and she asked him to follow her to a small outside booth so she could check her computer for prices. There it was—the offer we booked. The price was

$200. She led him to a spot where two SUVs sat side by side. Then, she asked which one he'd like to rent. She even indicated which would be better because one had GPS. He chose that one and followed her to her booth to complete the transaction. She told Chuck he'd have to confirm the contract at the main desk inside. It was all taken care of, and he could return to pick up the vehicle once confirmed. Easy peasy! But then came the shock from the inside desk.

Returning to the main desk, he met the same lady who'd talked with him from the start. He explained what had happened in the parking lot.

"We don't have outside desk personnel in the parking lot. And, parking lot attendants don't have the authority to rent vehicles and have no computer availability to our records. They can only give out keys and instructions to exit the lot."

Of course, my husband hadn't imagined the episode, nor did he fabricate the story. He asked that she look it up online to confirm the transaction. And, there it was—confirmed, $200.

Who was that lady in the parking lot? When

Chuck went out to pick up the vehicle, she was nowhere in sight. But she'd given him the keys when she completed the transaction. He drove the vehicle out of the parking lot! It was a done deal! It was a divine deal! I've often wondered whether God orchestrated this miracle with His angels. Could be! Nothing is impossible with God! What say you?

Take Shape

❖ **Verse to Ponder**:

"For we walk by faith, not by sight" (2 Corinthians 5:7).

❖ **Question:**

Can you believe God has the answer to the problems facing you today even though you can't see a positive outcome?

❖ **Today's Exercise:**

Memorizing. Educators have found that students who were required to memorize from an early age often go on to have more capacity to focus on educational tasks as high school and college students. It exercises their brains.

Memorizing Scripture turns our focus toward God—it exercises our souls. Scripture is at our command to recall it when we choose. Our faith grows, and our lives change as we shape our souls by memorizing Scripture.

Memorize God's Word so we move the mountain of impossibilities before us while focusing on Him and His promises. By memorizing Scripture, we exercise our brain and recall His truth when we face impossible situations. We envision God's plans and watch miracles unfold. We believe anything is possible—even angel encounters in rental car parking lots.

God's Funny Bone

Elbow Exercises for
Your Soul's Funny Bone

We were on home assignment in Pennsylvania, awaiting news of the approaching birth of our first granddaughter in Fairfax, Virginia, a few hundred miles away. Our bags packed, we hoped to arrive at our daughter and son-in-law's home a few days before the birth. But a phone call in the early evening caused us to begin our three-hour trip earlier than expected. Kayla was on the way two weeks ahead of schedule. We arrived at the hospital in time to greet our first granddaughter a few minutes after she entered our world. Grandparents will attest that this is a glorious occasion comparable to no other. After cuddling that precious, tiny baby for the first time, we gathered our belongings and headed to our daughter's home to get some much-needed rest at midnight—leaving baby and mother to rest for the night.

Panic and Fear

We snuggled into a soft, cozy bed and fell asleep. Suddenly, a noise awoke us at 2:00 A.M. Chad was rushing out the door and yelled for us to call Kristen and she would explain. It felt like our hearts stopped and dropped to the floor. We made the call.

Kristen explained that after we'd left the hospital, she began asking to see the baby. Hours went by, and still, they hadn't brought the baby to her. Almost frantic at 2:00 A.M., Kristen slipped out of bed and scoured the halls to find a nurse. She arrived at the nursery and saw Kayla in a corner separated from the other babies. She cried out for anyone to help her. The nurse heard her cry and ran to her side. She explained that Kayla had stopped breathing but had been revived and was being moved to the Neonatal Intensive Care Unit (NICU). The nurse escorted Kristen with the baby to the NICU, where they hooked her up to machines to help her breathe.

At the time of Kayla's birth, I wasn't the person you would have wanted at your side when in need of comfort and encouragement. I've grown in my faith since then, but I am still not anxious to be in circumstances that require one to hold back tears. Example, when Kristen was three years old, she fell out of bed and broke her collarbone. I awoke to the shrill scream, flew out of bed, hit the doorway and passed out. My husband faced a wife on the floor and a child in need—he rushed to care for our daughter— a difficult decision, but the one I would have wanted him to make. After all, I wasn't going anywhere. So now, I faced this sad situation with Kayla and wondered how I'd hold up for Kristen when everything inside me was coming apart.

Rushing In

Early the next morning, we rushed to the hospital. Exiting the elevator, my husband stopped at the desk but not me, I bolted down the hall to the room where Kristen had been the day before. The door was wide open. I stood there in the doorway confused. My daughter's face seemed changed, but still pretty. And, *who* was that man sitting beside her bed and holding her hand? I lingered somewhere between the twilight zone and planet earth.

"May we help you?" the man said in a cordial manner. I re-entered earth's atmosphere but still hadn't touched down. Looking at my daughter in the bed once again, I wanted to run. This young lady had an uncanny resemblance to my daughter, but she wasn't my daughter. I was frozen in time and wanted to melt into a puddle. It wasn't my daughter or my son-in-law. Mercy, I had entered the birthing room where my daughter gave birth the day before. Another couple occupied the room for the arrival of their baby. My daughter had been moved to her room.

After gathering my dignity from a far-off place, I apologized for my intrusion into their privacy. They politely carried on a conversation as though we were old friends meeting in a restaurant and talking about the menu. What extraordinary people who seemed more concerned about my embarrassment than their privacy.

After one more, "I'm so sorry," I exited the room and headed to find my husband—who hadn't a clue about my disappearance or whereabouts. I realized why he'd stopped at the desk. Of course, he inquired about the location of our daughter's room. He knew she would not be in the birthing room of the day before. Could I be any more humiliated at this moment? I could almost hear my husband's chuckle when he'd hear the story of my humiliation.

Eventually, we found each other in my daughter's new location and went to see baby Kayla. Wonderful nurses attended to her every need. As I put on the gown, the nurse helped me wiggle into it and asked if I was okay. I just couldn't stop crying when I looked at that beautiful baby with all the machines and needles helping her to breathe. "She's doing well, and we're doing tests to find her problem," she kindly said. How these "nurse-angels" do their job is beyond my comprehension. It takes a special person to be a nurse! Thank God for them.

My Other Daughter

That evening, we returned to visit our daughter and baby Kayla again. We just couldn't stay away. It relieved our minds to see Kristen sitting up in bed and smiling. Kayla continued to improve but still no results of the tests. Our son-in-law pulled up two chairs for us, and we plopped down with a sigh. Our weary bodies relaxed a bit. Everyone had a good laugh at my expense recounting my revisit to the birthing room. My daughter asked how my "other" daughter was doing. I joined in the joking, although a bit reluctantly.

I noticed the curtain for the second bed was drawn, and just as I was about to ask if Kristen had a roommate, the curtain flew open and so did my jaw. Any guesses who emerged from behind the curtain? Yep, the young couple from the birthing room and their parents. The laughter could be heard all the way down the hall and to the NICU where Kayla must have needed a laugh too.

The new mothers recounted their plan. "We wanted to put your 'other daughter' in my bed," Kristen explained. "We'd have loved to see your face when you walked into the room. But we thought you might have needed to be resuscitated, and we didn't want the nurses to have to add another bed to our room." And, as we all talked and laughed, our new friends told of their mutual faith of our loving and sometimes funny Savior.

Kayla continued to improve, and test results revealed she had been born with pneumonia. With antibiotics and lots and lots of love, she soon recovered and went home seven days after her birth. You can imagine how thankful we were to God for bringing us through such a harrowing time and as only He can, with some laughter along the way to relieve the stress and turn our eyes to Him in the middle of traumatic circumstances. God has a funny bone, too! Can't you imagine His beaming smile as He laughed along with us?

Take Shape

❖ **Verse to Ponder:**
    "Lift your praising hands to the Holy Place and bless God. In turn, may God of Zion bless you—God who made heaven and earth" (Psalm 134:2-3 MSG).

❖ Question:

How's the funny bone of your soul? Is it broken or bruised?

❖ Today's exercise:

Elbow stretches will restore movement to the elbow after an injury. So how do we restore our funny bone that runs alongside our elbow when it is injured. Do we stretch it too? Yes!

Did you know that your funny bone is actually a nerve, not a bone? It's the ulnar nerve. The funny bone got its nickname because of the funny feeling you get when you hit it. It doesn't hurt but instead gives you that funny feeling—not pain, not actual tingling, just a funny feeling. You get that funny feeling when you hit the humerus—the long bone that starts at your elbow and goes up to your shoulder. The ulnar nerve lets your brain know about feelings in your fourth and fifth fingers and controls some movement of your hand. The funny bone in your arm can't break because it is a nerve not a bone. But the funny bone of our soul can break.

The good news is God can heal it and restore our sense of humor. God elbows us with His humor to let the funny bone of our souls tingle again after an injury.

Elbow soul-stretches with God move the mountain of soul trauma. They restore our soul's funny bone and stretch our sense of humor. Stretch your physical elbows and funny bone to heaven, lift your hands in praise to Him, and let His humor tickle your soul's funny bone.

God's Messengers
Say Goodbye to Your Flabby Soul

Life is full of endings and beginnings—goodbyes and hellos, relocations of homes and jobs, temporary separations and permanent loss. All these circumstances evoke emotions—sad and happy ones. I often wonder why God called me (a homebody who looks for ways to escape goodbyes) to be a missionary. As a child, I couldn't leave my house for a sleepover at my best friend's house, and she lived only five doors away. And here I am, a missionary with a life of goodbyes and travel, having spent thirty-seven years sleeping 6,000 miles from what used to be home.

There's only one explanation—God.

Allow me to share one last myth with you—missionaries don't possess special powers and extinguished emotions for the task of leaving behind loved ones, a comfortable life, and the blessings of their home country. They cry just like you would if you left it all behind. As I contemplated writing the final chapter of this book, memories of the beginning chapter of my faith journey ignited a spark in my soul.

Missionaries in Your Neighborhood

My journey of faith began when I met my neighbors, Joanne and Fuzzy. If you think you must leave your home country to be a missionary, meet Joanne and Fuzzy—neighbors who lived on the street where I grew up and where my husband and I bought our first house. We'd known of them our entire lives—all twenty-three years at the time—but never knew them personally until we moved next door to them.

We immediately formed a friendship. Soon, fresh baked cookies arrived at our kitchen door by way of their daughters, Debbie and Lori. Next, their sons, Scott and Tim, would volunteer to cut grass or shovel snow. Fuzzy would invite us to church and give us *Our Daily Bread* devotionals along with Bible verses and words of encouragement. They even invited us to their lovely cabin for weekends. We'd been married four years but never had neighbors like them— friendly, loving, and generous. There was something different and wonderful about this family. What was it?

Joanne exemplified a loving, devoted wife and mother; she quickly became my role model and mentor. But what she taught me through her everyday life one day changed my life. She talked about God a lot and sparked my curiosity about the God she served fervently. I wondered what made her so passionate. Joanne had something I didn't have—but wanted.

God wasn't a stranger to me or to my husband. We went to church regularly, and my husband also had a deep devotion to God that I lacked. I wanted to discover the mystery of this difference.

A Gum-and-Life-Savers Friend

One day Joanne gave me a gift. It was the Bible, but only the New Testament. I had no idea of the Gift inside those pages that awaited me. That afternoon, I sat in my living room and read the Book from cover to cover in a few hours and received the best gift possible—eternal life. I have never been the same since. I met Jesus on those pages. The Bible says, "For God so loved the world that he gave his one and only son, that whosoever believes in him shall not perish but have eternal life" (John 3:16 KJV). God's Son, Jesus, became real to me that day.

Joanne left this earth too soon, but Fuzzy carried on their ministry until he joined her there on that beautiful shore in heaven. While he waited to join Joanne, Fuzzy continued to work for the Lord. He never hesitated to tell of his wonderful Savior and Lord. He blessed us and taught us to serve the Lord as he did—with all his heart and soul. He prayed faithfully for us every day and for our ministry in Bolivia.

Fuzzy will be remembered by many for his special ministry—delivering *Our Daily Bread* devotionals to mailboxes all over our home area for many decades. And, he had a unique ministry with the kids in our area of Bolivia. He sent gum and Life

Savers candy with us in our luggage for the kids in our classes.

He'd always say, "We want you to have this gift for the kids in Bolivia. We love you, but not as much as Jesus loves you." "We" meant, he and Joanne. I will never forget him saying that every time we said goodbye. Then he'd say, "Now tell the kids Jesus loves them."

During our furloughs, we had many breakfast times at McDonald's with Fuzzy. Joanne loved McDonald's—so do I. Joanne and Fuzzy live forever in heaven now—maybe eating a hamburger at McDonald's together (inserting a bit of imagination here). We all miss them. But because they shared Jesus with their neighbors, my husband and I will be there with them for all eternity. And because they were Jesus' messengers, many in Bolivia also hear the Good News. Fuzzy and Joanne were missionaries to Bolivia without applying for a passport or boarding a plane. They were God's messengers where they lived and worked.

Building into the Lives Around Us

How thankful we are for all who support and pray for us and for God's work in Bolivia. God's messengers work all around the world—in every nook and cranny of His tiny towns, big cities, and yes, the ends of the earth.

God gave me the desire to be a missionary from the first time I heard a missionary speak in our church, and He eventually led Chuck and me to Bolivia to tell others about Jesus on the foreign field—God's messengers. What a privilege for us!

Now I have neighbors of a different color, a different language, and a different culture. Yet I desire to be a neighbor like Joanne and Fuzzy were to me, with a passion for souls and a desire to share Christ with those who don't know Him yet. I have a ministry with teen girls. I teach cooking and baking, and in each class, I teach the girls about God and the Bible. Joanne taught me many of the things I know about baking, cooking, and God. I like to think that God lets her share the joy in heaven, somehow, when souls are saved through our ministry. I know she'd be happy to see how she influenced my life and how I am now using those skills to reach young girls for Christ in Bolivia.

All Hellos; No Goodbyes

It's wonderful to have assurance that one day we will live with Jesus in heaven forever, and we will be reunited with those loved ones who have gone on before us.

Heaven is a real place that God has created especially for those who believe His Word and trust Jesus as Savior. And, there will be no goodbyes in heaven. I know I will see Fuzzy and Joanne again. Will I see you there? I hope so.

Over my years of growing in Christ, God has shown me that this mountain of goodbyes that I face can be moved because He desires to use me to take His message to the lost. He can move your mountains too, whatever they may be.

Take Shape

- ❖ **Verse to Ponder:**

    "You've been raised on the **Message** of the faith and have followed sound teaching. Now pass on this counsel to the followers of Jesus there, and you'll be a good servant of Jesus. Stay clear of silly stories that get dressed up as religion. **Exercise** daily in God—no spiritual flabbiness, please! Workouts in the gymnasium are useful, but a disciplined life in God is far more so, making you **fit** both today and forever. You can count on this. Take it to heart. This is why we've thrown ourselves into this venture so totally. We're banking on the living God, Savior of all men and women, especially believers" (1 Timothy 4:6-10 MSG).

- ❖ **Question:**

    Are you a messenger who exercises your faith to spread God's message or do you need to exercise your faith and believe the message that Jesus loves you?

❖ **Today's Exercise:**
Faith Exercises will shape your soul for the work before you. Exercising your faith in Jesus guarantees you a home in heaven forever. Exercise daily with God by reading His Word and applying it to your life so your soul won't be flabby.

Faith Exercises with God will move the mountains that block us from taking the message of the gospel to the world both near and far. When we continue to shape our souls for the job before us, they stay fit and don't become flabby. We can say *goodbye* to our flabby souls. We will build up our souls and the souls of the body of Christ. Let's keep our souls in shape by doing a plethora of faith exercises to shape our souls and be fit to get God's message out. The day is near when our work will end, and we'll fly to heaven—no more goodbyes only hellos, hallelujahs, and the beginning of eternity in heaven. Imagine exercising in heaven with no pain and all the gain—eternal perfect bodies just like Jesus. Now's the time to work out and stay fit spiritually by exercising our souls until that day when we turn in our membership to God's Gym and trade it for a crown in God's Heaven. Because we trust in the Savior, we are now and will forever be members of God's family. Our souls can get in shape and stay fit until that day because of Jesus' exercise of love. Whether we are missionaries with or without a passport, we all can be missionaries who mirror Joanne and Fuzzy—telling our neighbors far and near, "Jesus loves you!"

I'm looking forward to the day I'll be with Jesus and all my eternity neighbors—forever. Until then, let's keep working out our faith to shape our souls for eternity's purpose.

References

"Machine Guns and Sleeping Ghosts" first appeared in *Angels, Miracles, and Heavenly Encounters,* Bethany House Publishers, 2012. Used by permission. All rights reserved.

"I Like Jesus" first appeared in *Grandparenting Through Obstacles,* Reneé Gray-Wilburn, Dianne E Butts, Pix-N-Pens Publishing, 2012. Used by permission. All rights reserved.

"In My Grandmother's Eyes" first appeared in *Grandmother, Mother, and Me,* Editor Donna Clark Goodrich, Hidden Brook Press, 2012. Used by permission. All rights reserved.

"Freaky Face" first appeared in *I Believe in Miracles,* Cecil Murphey & Twila Belk Regal/Gospel Light, 2013. Used by permission. All rights reserved.

"Why We Need Underwear Friends" first appeared in *Just Between Us: Encouraging and Equipping Women for a Life of Faith,* Fall 2012. Just Between Us, 777 S. Barker Road, Brookfield, WI 53045. Used by permission. All rights reserved.

About the Author

Peggy Cunningham and her husband, Chuck have been missionaries in Bolivia, South America, since 1981. In 1999, they founded Rumi Rancho Ministries. Rumi Rancho is their ministry base and home outside the city of Cochabamba where they work with the Quechua people and have a children's ministry. They also work with national churches.

As a writer, Peggy's been published in anthologies, Christian magazines, and online publications. Her heart for children and vibrant imagination led the way to write her first picture book series, ***Really Rare Rabbits***: Books 1-3. Peggy's most recent series, ***Hooray for Holidays***: Books 1-4 was inspired by the real-life animals of Rumi Rancho. She also writes non-fiction devotionals for adults of all ages. ***Dancing Like Bees***, and ***Shape Your Soul*** are Peggy's latest devotionals. All books are available on Amazon.com.

Visit Peggy on the Web:
www.PeggyCunningham.com

Other Books by the Author

**Dancing Like Bees:
31 Steps to De-Stress, Delight, and Dance Like Bees**

God has a reset button for our souls.

Frustrated and exhausted, Peggy walked the mission property early mornings to slip away temporarily from her caregiver duties and meet with her Savior. Her husband suffered from a bout with shingles that left him in constant pain with no relief—not even with morphine. Months turned into years. Countless doctors tried their best with no success.

Where was God? Didn't He see them in the middle of a foreign country with no help? Hadn't they given their lives to serve as missionaries and trusted Him for their health? She wept as she sat near a flowerbed filled with daises. Just then, the buzz of bees drew her attention. They flew peacefully from flower to flower doing the job God created them to do, even as a storm approached.

Through the thirty-one devotions, this book examines what Peggy learned about God's intricate creation of the honeybee and how it speaks direction into our need for living peaceful, productive lives while overcoming stress and achieving joy. God is faithful always, and His creation magnifies His majesty if we take time to seek Him in everyday situations—even through the honeybee.

<u>Now Available on Amazon.</u>

The Really Rare Rabbit Series
Picture Books for Children

in English and in Spanish

Available on Amazon

in Print and on Kindle

https://amzn.to/2YvV0Xi

Visit Peggy's Amazon Page

https://amzn.to/2TAnfk4

**Thank you
for reading our books!**

**Look for other books
published by**